U

C

Makin

With an

THIS BOOK IS TO BE RETURNED ON OR BEFORE THE
LAST DATE STAMPED BELOW OTR

green books

First published in 2008 by

Green Books
Foxhole, Dartington
Totnes, Devon TQ9 6EB
www.greenbooks.co.uk

© Bish Muir 2008

Designed by Stephen Prior

Printed in the UK by Cambrian Printers. The text paper is made from 100% recycled post-consumer waste, and the covers from 75% recycled material.

DISCLAIMER: The advice in this book is believed to be correct at the time of printing, but the authors and publishers accept no liability for actions inspired by this book.

ISBN 978 1 900322 30 0

Contents

Introduction

Introduction

Nobody likes throwing away good food – quite apart from anything else, it is a terrible waste of money, as well as very harmful to the environment. However, with a little bit of guidance and inspiration we can all cut back on the amount of food waste we produce, and work towards having a guilt-free kitchen!

Cooking from leftovers came naturally to those who lived during the time of post-war rationing. They developed incredible powers of resourcefulness when it came to cooking, and would baulk at the idea of wasting 'good food' when it was hard to come by.

Further back in history we find an even more resourceful bunch than our grandmothers and great grandmothers: the 'bijoutiers' who emerged in Paris and Versailles in the eighteenth and nineteenth centuries. They would go around to the grand houses, hotels and restaurants in the city, and collect the leftover food in big baskets. Much of the food would have been totally untouched and, once collected, the food could be rearranged on little plates and sold at the markets and even back into restaurants! The name 'bijoutiers' comes from the fact that the food was arranged on the plate to look like 'bijoux' – 'little jewels'.

Unfortunately these resourceful skills have not always been passed down through the generations and we now live in a largely 'throw away' society. Excessive food waste is an even greater problem now than it was back in the eighteenth and nineteenth centuries because it is no longer restricted to the privileged classes.

Today food is more plentiful, but there is no reason why using our leftovers should be considered a dying skill. Cooking ingredients have never been so accessible to us, and with a stock of simple ingredients in the cupboard, great results can be achieved.

In the UK we throw away a third of the food we buy – 6.7 million tonnes every year

The unpalatable facts

- Of the 6.7 million tonnes of food that are thrown away every year in the UK, 4.1 million tonnes is unopened and untouched. Of this, 340,000 tonnes is still 'in date'. This is largely a result of a lack of meal planning, but also of over-supply – 1.2 million tonnes of food waste is simply left on our plates!

- In 2006 the World Food Programme provided 730,000 tonnes of food aid to the Darfur region of Sudan for refugees (source: World Food Programme); that is one ninth of the 6.7 million tonnes we in the UK throw away every year.

- The average household throws away between £15,000 and £24,000 worth of food in a lifetime – up to £610 per household per year.

- Nobody likes throwing away food – in a recent survey, 68% of people who admitted to throwing away food cared about it, because they viewed it as a waste of money as well as a waste of good food.

- Food waste is increasing at a rate of 15% every decade.

- Every year we throw away 5.1 million whole potatoes, 2.8 million whole tomatoes, 1 million slices of ham and 1.2 million sausages. Rather than throwing them away, these should be considered 'gems' as they can provide the basis for so many delicious meals, for example soups, stir-fries and omelettes.

We can do something about it!

Whether you have a household of fussy eaters or live on your own, this book will help you reduce the amount of food you throw away, save money and do your bit to protect the environment at the same time.

The average household throws away between £15,000 and £24,000 worth of food in a lifetime – up to £610 per household per year.

Whether our incentive is to save the environment or the money in our wallets, the government has made a commitment to reduce food waste in landfill to 35% of 1995 levels by 2020, which means we all have to do our bit.

Why should we reduce our food waste?

Rotting food buried in landfill sites generates methane, a greenhouse gas over twenty times more potent than carbon dioxide and a major contributor to climate change.

So serious is the problem, in fact, that it is estimated that if we stopped throwing away food that could be eaten, we could make carbon savings equivalent to taking one in five cars off the road!

In addition to producing methane, rotting food in landfill sites also produces leachate, a liquid produced when water (from rain) passes through the waste. The leachates collect at the base of the landfill and are a potentially hazardous waste, causing pollution to groundwater and the environment, which can cause health problems.

As well as the above, it is an uncomfortable fact that while we waste millions of tonnes of perfectly edible food, people are still dying of hunger in the third world.

Whether our incentive is to save the environment or the money in our wallets, the government has made a commitment to reduce food waste in landfill to 35% of 1995 levels by 2020, which means we all have to do our bit. Reducing food waste is one of a number of really practical ways in which we can help slow down climate change, and if it reduces our shopping bills and produces tasty results then we're all quids in!

Essential tools of the trade

You don't need a kitchen that is stuffed full of electrical gadgets and trendy gismos to produce fabulous meals, but there are a few 'must-have' items which will give you the equipment you need to make the most of the recipes in this book.

- *Bottle opener* – **a great accompaniment for every good cook!**

- *Can opener* – **one that fixes to the wall is the best option.**

- *Cheese grater* – **try and get one that comes with a sealable container so that you can store any leftover grated cheese easily.**

- *Heavy casserole dish* – **ideal for cooking soups and stews on the top of the stove and finishing off slowly in the oven.**

- *Food processor/liquidiser* – **very useful for making soups and smoothies.**

- *Microwave* – **not essential but, for ease and speed, very handy for reheating leftovers.**

- *Plastic clips* – **these prevent spillage and keep things fresh for longer; clothes pegs or elastic bands do the same job.**

- *Pyrex dishes* – **very useful when microwaving food, or reheating in the oven.**

- *Selection of airtight containers* – **empty ice cream containers will do, but there is nothing to beat those with a special rubber seal, which keep leftovers really fresh and avoids contamination and nasty smells in your fridge.**

- *Sharp knife* – **essential for preparing food easily.**

- *Weighing scales* – **essential for getting the correct amounts of ingredients.**

- *Wooden knife block or knife magnet* – **a good way to store your knives as it protects the blades and makes them easy to find.**

- *Wooden spoons* – **for using with a non-stick pan.**

- *Wok or large non-stick frying pan* – **stir-fries and quick curries are a good way to use up a single carrot, onion, etc.**

It is essential to keep all kitchen equipment really clean and stored in a place that is both easy to get at and safe from dirt and children.

'Must-have' ingredients in the store cupboard

There are a number of ingredients that come up time and again in cooking, and they form the backbone of your recipes. They are there to provide flavour and substance, and even if it appears that the cupboard is completely empty, as long as you keep these vital ingredients stocked up at all times, you will be able to create something – however basic.

Many of the items in the list below will store well, so you can afford to buy a reasonable quantity without fear of it going off or getting stale, provided it is stored correctly. This is a perfect example of where storage containers and clips can be so useful for storing opened food and half-empty packets.

- *Baked beans* – **a very good source of protein and great for an instant meal.**

- *Dried fruits* – **these last for months, if sealed, and can be chopped up and added to cereal, curries or puddings or just eaten on their own as a mid-morning snack.**

- *Eggs* – **whether it's Spanish omelettes, simple cakes or just scrambled egg on toast, it's always good to have half a dozen eggs in the house. Free-range eggs definitely taste better and have beautiful deep orange yolks that add colour to your cooking.**

- *Flour (plain and self-raising)* – **essential for sauces, e.g. cheese sauce for macaroni cheese, and for baking.**

- *Garlic bulbs* – **garlic enhances any number of savoury dishes – from stir-fries and sauces to pies and salad dressings – and is easily stored in a cool place.**

- *Herbs and spices* – **as well as a few fresh herbs the following dried herbs are very useful: basil, oregano, rosemary, tarragon, mint, parsley, thyme, marjoram and mixed herbs. Useful spices include ground ginger, ground coriander, nutmeg, chilli powder and curry powder.**

- *Lemon juice* – **a bottle of lemon juice is always useful to have as it can jazz up puddings, sauces and stir-fries.**

- *Nuts* – **an assortment of nuts can be added to cakes, stir-fries and are a very good source of protein. Stored in a sealed bag or container, they will last for months.**

- *Rice or pasta* – **rice or pasta dishes, using left-over meat, vegetables and cheese, are easy to rustle up, and both of these staples store very well.**

- *Oils* – **whilst a good vegetable or sunflower oil is essential for frying food, olive oil, although more expensive, is delicious for salad dressings. Sesame oil is fantastic for stir-fries as it has a rich, nutty taste.**

- *Onions* – **essential for any casserole or sauce, and will add taste to just about anything. Store them in a dry, cool place and they will last for several weeks.**

- *Ready-made sauces* – **always good to have in the cupboard for adding to leftover meat or vegetables.**

- *Seasoning* – **sugar, salt, pepper and mustard.**

- *Soy sauce* – **great for adding to stir-fries.**

- *Stock cubes* – **you can make your own stock from meat or chicken carcasses, but stock cubes are quick and easy to use, and are great for making simple soups. Vegetable stock cubes help to add real flavour in a leftover vegetable soup, or when used in a risotto instead of water.**

- *Tinned tomatoes* – **these are one of the basic ingredients for pasta sauces and soups and will obviously store for months.**

- *Tinned pulses* – **chickpeas, butter beans, haricot beans and lentils add substance and flavour to soups and stews.**

- *Tinned tuna* – **fabulous with a baked potato and mayonnaise, for spicing up a salad or adding to a pasta sauce.**

- *Tinned soup* – **either for a quick meal or to add to casseroles, e.g. adding chicken and mushroom soup to a casserole.**

- *Tomato purée* – **always good to add to bolognaise sauce or shepherd's/cottage pie to give it a tomato taste. Also great in tomato soup or stews and casseroles.**

- *Vinegar* – **useful for making salad dressings and for making pickles or chutney.**

- *Worcestershire sauce* – **delicious with beef dishes such as cottage pie and bolognaise.**

'Must-have' ingredients in the fridge

- *Butter or margarine* – **features in so many leftover recipes as it forms the basis of any sauce or cake mix.**

- *Crème fraîche or fromage frais* – **stir into pasta sauces or risottos for a creamy taste. Use in quiches. Also great on fruit puddings and pies.**

- *Cheese* – **a good hunk of mature Cheddar adds taste and substance to many dishes. Keep the cheese wrapped up in greaseproof paper to avoid it drying out. If you get a bit of mould on the edges, just cut it off – it won't affect the rest of the cheese.**

- *Houmous* – **great as a dip for sliced up leftover raw vegetables or pitta bread.**

- *Mayonnaise* – **always keep a jar in the fridge. It lasts for ages and goes with chicken, potatoes, tuna and just about anything that fits inside a sandwich!**

- *Milk* – **even if you don't have it on your cereal or in tea and coffee, it is essential for making white sauces and many puddings.**

- *Pastry* – **some ready made shortcrust or puff pastry is always useful. If you don't want to use it immediately, store it in the freezer and bring it out in good time so that it thaws properly before being used.**

- *Pesto* – **lasts for ages in the fridge and is delicious with pasta or plopped on top of a risotto or salad. Top up the pot with some olive oil if it starts to dry out.**

- *Taramasalata* – **like houmous it provides a delicious snack with sliced up raw vegetables.**

- *Yoghurt* – **can be added to many sauces or just poured over fruit or sweet puddings. Natural yoghurt can be a substitute for cream in many dishes e.g. curries and casseroles.**

Planning your shopping

- A third of us go shopping without a list.

- In a recent survey 22% of people who were asked why they threw away so much food, said that it was because they bought too much.

- Another 22% claimed they were tempted by multi-packs but then did not plan their week's meals, so that the extra food remained unused and had to be thrown away.

- 34% admitted to throwing away food because it had gone past the 'use-by' or 'best before' date.

- Research shows that people who plan their weekly shop are less likely to buy too much and so less inclined to throw away unwanted or unused food.

Keep an eye on 'use-by' dates

It is a good idea to plan your weekly menus by the 'use by' dates on the food you buy. Obviously, something with a shorter shelf life should be used early on, with any leftovers being used to create a stir-fry or soup for later in the week.

Make the most of what you buy

Here is an example of good planning which gets the most out of your food and makes your money go further: buy a whole chicken together with some vegetables, cook it to have a roast on one day and then strip the carcass to use the remaining meat for a risotto or other chicken dish in a couple of days time, and use the bones for stock.

Menu planning example:

Sunday: Large roast chicken, roast potatoes, carrots and peas. Strip chicken carcass and make and freeze stock from the bones and any leftover vegetables.

Monday: Chicken sandwiches for school/work packed lunch, and risotto for evening meal using leftover peas and some mushrooms with plenty of Parmesan.

Tuesday: Use up leftover roast potatoes by slicing and frying them. Serve with sausages and vegetables.

Wednesday: Chicken Crunch (p.102) using rest of cold chicken.

Thursday: Chicken soup made with stock made on Sunday. The soup will freeze well for another occasion.

Buy in season

If you can, buy local food that is in season. Not only is it much fresher and tastier (having not been chilled and shipped or flown half way around the world to get to the supermarket shelves), but it is generally cheaper. Ordering an organic vegetable box is a good way to ensure you are eating locally produced, seasonal vegetables. There are a number of companies doing these, e.g. Riverford, Abel & Cole and The Organic Delivery Company. You can also buy fresh produce (often organic) from your local farmers' market.

Avoid 'BOGOFs' which don't store easily

BOGOF (Buy One Get One Free) offers are fine if it is something like mince that can go straight into the freezer, but with perishable food that won't freeze it isn't good value if the 'free' item goes mouldy before you get around to eating it. Be realistic about what you can eat in a week (or next few days) before you buy – good planning saves you having to throw away food that you simply have not managed to get around to eating.

Don't shop when you're hungry

The best way to avoid buying too much food is to make sure you avoid shopping when you're feeling really hungry, as any planning may go completely out of the window! Shopping without children, if at all possible, is also a good idea as it helps you to concentrate and plan.

If you can, buy local food that is in season.

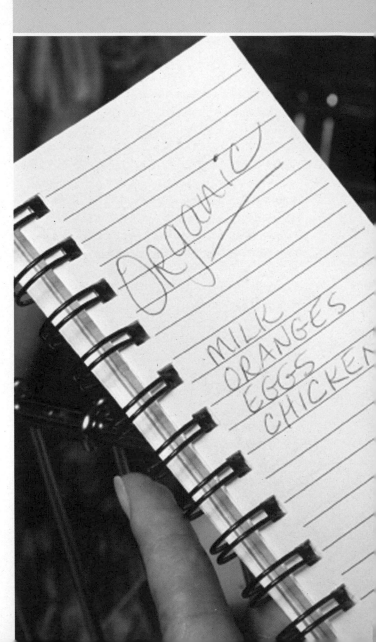

Storing leftovers

Care must be taken when storing leftovers – here are a few basic rules:

- Always let cooked food cool down fully before it is put in the fridge.

- Don't leave food out overnight, as this can cut its shelf life significantly.

- Different foods should be prepared and stored separately. To prevent the spread of bacteria, raw meat should be stored on the bottom shelf of the fridge (or in a tightly sealed container) so that it doesn't drip on to other food. Meat and dairy should be stored on separate shelves wherever possible.

- Keep your fridge at the right temperature: between 1° and 5°C is the optimum. It's a good idea to buy a magnetic fridge thermometer for the inside of your fridge.

- If you cook more than you need, freeze what is left over in an airtight container for using another time.

- If you have an abundance of soft fruit, then either open freeze it on trays before bagging up or putting in containers, or make it into a simple chutney or jam.

- Few people have the luxury of a cool larder or dairy, so there can be occasions when the fridge gets rather over-full. This can be avoided with careful planning: make sure you don't take up valuable fridge space with things that don't necessarily need to be in a cool environment.

- Having said that, it can be useful to use a shelf in the door of the fridge to store leftover 'bits' such as half an onion or lemon, chunks of dried up cheese, half a courgette etc. Then when you are making a dish, it is easy check whether you can add any of these 'bits' to your cooking.

- Many packaged or tinned foods carry storage instructions, so it's a good idea to read these carefully.

Storage times for most common leftovers

Food	How to store?	Maximum storage time	Freezing?
Cooked meat	Preferably leave on the bone to avoid drying out. Cover with foil. Alternatively strip meat from the bone and wrap well in foil. Store in fridge.	2-3 days	YES
Cooked chicken or turkey	As above. Store in fridge.	2-3 days	YES
Cooked fish	Cover with foil. Store in fridge.	1-2 days	YES
Cooked vegetables	Plastic containers or cover with clingfilm. Store in fridge. Peas, beans, onions and potatoes (not mashed) freeze well.	3-5 days	SOME
Cooked stews and casseroles	Cover well with foil or store in dish with lid. Store in fridge.	2-4 days	YES
Milk puddings or custard	Cover with clingfilm. Store in fridge.	2-3 days	NO
Raw fruit salad	Cover with clingfilm. Store in fridge.	3-4 days	NO
Grated cheese	Sealed container. Store in fridge.	10-14 days	YES
Egg whites	In covered container in fridge.	1-2 days	YES
Egg yolks	In covered container in fridge.	3-4 days	NO
Breadcrumbs	Sealed plastic bag. Store in fridge.	3 weeks	YES

Reheat food to at least 180°C to kill off any bacteria that may have formed.

Reheating food

It is extremely important to reheat leftover food properly but remember that it should only be reheated, not re-cooked or you will lose the goodness from the food. The best way to reheat food is to put it on full heat in the microwave as this will heat it from the inside out. If you don't have a microwave, then reheat the food to at least 180°C to kill off any bacteria that may have formed (see recipes for timings).

A tip for meat is to slice, mince or cube it before reheating to ensure it heats evenly throughout.

'Use-by' dates and other instructions

What the terms mean:

'Use-by'

This means exactly that. Officially, food and drink should not be consumed after the end of the 'use-by' date shown on the label. With meat and fish this is definitely the case, even if it may smell and look fine. Although officially dairy should also not be used after the 'use-by' date, slightly off milk is perfect for making scones and will not make you ill; and within reason, cheese can still be eaten even when there is a little mould on it, provided you remove the mould.

Remember that 'use-by' dates are only applicable if the storage instructions on the label are adhered to, as otherwise food might go off before its 'use-by' date.

'Sell-by' or 'Display until'

These are instructions for shop staff to tell them when they should take a product off the shelves; they do not mean that the food cannot be eaten after that date. In fact, one manufacturer of yoghurts, Stonyfield Farm, actually states on its website "It can be perfectly okay to eat yoghurt after the sell-by date. Just use your judgement. If the yoghurt looks, smells, and tastes good, and there are no visible signs of mould, it's okay to eat."

'Best before'

Eggs should not be eaten after the 'best before' date, or if the shells are cracked. 'Best before' is usually applied to foods that last longer, such as tinned food or frozen or dried food such as pasta. It should be safe to eat food after the 'best before' date, but the food will no longer be at its best and may begin to lose its flavour and texture.

The best thing to do is to plan your menus around the dates on the food, so that if you know that something is coming up to the end of its life you can make sure you eat it on or before that day.

Composting

Up to a third of our household waste can be composted

Composting your fruit and vegetable peelings, apple cores, tea bags, egg shells etc., rather than putting them in the bin, reduces the amount of rotting food in landfill sites. You don't need a big garden to do this.

There are some fantastic wormeries and mini compost systems on the market that will sit comfortably on a patio or balcony, and children love wormeries – there is something fascinating about watching the worms at work! Most council websites will tell you how to get hold of compost bins and wormeries, and many will be able to offer them at reduced prices. In addition, many councils have set up local community-based composting schemes where people can take their food waste and other compostables to a communal site and, in return, buy the resulting compost back to put on their gardens.

There are many benefits of composting. Not only do you reduce your waste but you are producing fantastic nutrient-rich compost for your gardens or pot plants.

You can easily compost:

- **Fruit and vegetables and their peelings**

- **Tea bags and tea leaves, coffee grounds**

- **Cardboard, e.g. cut-up cereal packets and egg boxes**

- **Egg shells (crushed)**

You need a sealed composting system to compost:

- **Meat**
- **Fish**
- **Cooked food**

You can't compost these safely:

- **Cat litter**
- **Dog faeces**

Keep waste food out of landfill by composting it.

Save waste – buy the exact amount of loose perishables that you need, rather than pre-packaged.

Packaging

It's generally best to buy food loose where possible rather than pre-packaged, because if you buy pre-packaged, you can't choose an exact amount and will often end up buying more than you need. Also, pre-packaged food will always cost more, as the cost of the packaging is passed on to the customer.

It is always a good idea to buy your perishable food loose, especially if you are only buying for one or two people. That way you are only buying what you think you need and are less likely to waste any – and you will save money. You will also reduce the amount of waste going to landfill.

However, there are ways in which you can make use of the packaging from supermarkets, for example:

- **Reuse plastic containers from tomatoes etc. for seed trays – perfect for growing herbs or cress.**

- **Reuse yoghurt pots for children's paint pots or for storing elastic bands etc.**

- **Reuse soup pots for freezing stock, or your home-made soup.**

- **Reuse ice cream containers for storing food or small toys.**

- **Collect your plastic containers or bottles, and give them to your local primary school for their art and craft lessons.**

The transportation of food around the world releases huge amounts of CO_2 into the atmosphere.

Food miles

Some grapes on our supermarket shelves have travelled over 7,000 miles from Chile, whilst apples from New Zealand may have travelled a staggering 10,000 miles.

By food miles, we mean the distance our food travels from its original growing place to our plates, including journeys made to be produced, processed, packaged and displayed in the shop. Large amounts of fuel are used to move the food from one place to the next, whether by air, sea or road, all of which has a huge impact on the environment.

We have already looked at the benefits to your wallet of buying food in season if you can, but if we want to protect the environment, it is important to consider how far food has travelled to get to our shops, and buy locally grown food in season whenever possible.

How to use this book

Leftovers can be divided into two types:

- **The cooked food that has been left after a meal or is simply unused due to bad planning. Although we tend to get more flavour from raw ingredients, cooked food can often be incorporated in addition to other raw ingredients.**

- **The uncooked leftover which takes the form of the single carrot, leek, parsnip, tomato, sausage, slice of ham or egg in the fridge or cupboard. These often get discarded because on their own they do not constitute a big enough portion to provide a meal for the household.**

The book is divided into three sections:

The A-Z

This features both types of leftover (see left) and gives you:

- **quick and easy recipes**
- **tips for using the leftover**
- **cross-references to the main recipes (both basic and individual – see below)**
- **other recipes in which you can use the leftover**

Basic Recipes

These are recipes that can be adapted according to the leftover, e.g. 'Basic Stock' or 'Basic Stir-fry'.

Individual Recipes

These are recipes which work best with specific leftover ingredients e.g. 'Bubble and Squeak', and 'Fish Cakes'.

Key to symbols used in the book

(U) Uncooked leftover – single item, or not enough to make a meal/last drops in the pot

(C) Cooked leftover

🕐 Time to prepare (in minutes)

🕐 Time to cook (in minutes)

A-Z of leftover ingredients

with quick and easy recipes and tips

A-Z of leftover ingredients
with quick and easy recipes

Unless specified, all recipes are for four servings.

APPLES (U)

RECIPES *Basic:* Chutney (p.56), Salad (pp.68-9), Crumble/Pie – Fruit (p.82), Fruit Salad (p.83), Pasties – Sweet (p.84), Smoothies (p.86), Stewed Fruit (p.88), Fruit and Vegetable Juices (pp.117-9). *Individual:* Apple and Cinnamon Fritters (p.154), Baked Apples and Pears (p.155).

Quick and easy
- Apple sauce – cook cored, peeled and chopped apple in a little water with a pinch of cinnamon and some lemon zest for about 10 minutes. Delicious with pork.
- If you're roasting pork, try adding 2 or 3 wrinkly apples, quartered and cored, with one red or Spanish onion, some fennel seeds and half a large glass measure of white wine to the same baking tray with the pork – makes delicious apple and onion confit.

Can also be used in
Pancake Fillings (pp.128-30), Mixed Fruit Cheesecake (p.170).

Tips
- Cheapest to buy English apples in late summer and autumn.

See also
PEARS.

APRICOTS (U)
RECIPES *Basic:* Chutney (p.56), Curry (p.58), Crumble/Pie – Fruit (p.82), Fruit Salad (p.83), Pasties – Sweet (p.84), Stewed Fruit (p.88). *Individual:* Coronation Turkey (p.107).

Quick and easy
- Chop apricots into little pieces and sprinkle on your cereal.

See also
BACON.

AUBERGINE (C/U)
RECIPES *Basic:* Chutney (p.56), Crumble/Pie – Vegetable (p.57). *Individual:* Ratatouille (p.135).

Quick and easy
- Simple Melanzana – fry up some sliced onion and garlic and add to sliced, grilled aubergine in an ovenproofed dish. Pour over a tin of chopped tomatoes, add some basil and thyme, top with grated Parmesan and bake in a moderate oven for 20 minutes.
- Serve cold, with cold roast beef or lamb.

Can also be used in
Roasted Vegetables (p.67).

AVOCADO (U)
RECIPES *Individual:* Guacamole (p.112).

Quick and easy
- Slice up and serve with sliced tomato and vinaigrette.

Tips
- To ripen avocados, put in a warm spot in a paper bag with a banana.
- Sprinkling with lemon/lime juice will prevent cut avocado from discolouration.

Can also be used in
Salad (pp.68-9).

BACON (C/U)

RECIPES *Basic:* Chicken/Turkey Pie (p.60), Quiche (p.64), Risotto (p.65). *Individual:* Baked Potato Fillings (pp.92-3), Bubble and Squeak (p.95), Cheesy Chicken Breasts (p.100), Chicken Liver and Wild Mushroom Pâté (p.103), Macaroni Cheese (p.124), Spanish Omelette (p.142), Stuffed Peppers with Rice (p.145).

Quick and easy

- Bacon sandwich with lettuce, tomatoes and mayonnaise.
- Chop up cooked bacon and sprinkle on salads, baked potatoes, pizzas.
- Wrap rashers of bacon round cocktail sausages, apricots or dates and cook in a hot oven for 15 minutes.

Tip

- If you are using bacon for stews or casseroles, then try buying 'bacon bits' or 'cooking bacon' from your butcher or supermarket, these are the misshapen bacon bits left over after the bacon rashers are cut and are half the price of bacon rashers but just as tasty.

Can also be used in

Salad (pp.68-9), Sauce – White (p.70).

See also

BEEF, BROAD BEANS, CAULIFLOWER, CHICKEN, CRÈME FRAÎCHE, DATES, EGGS, LEEKS, ONIONS (RED).

BAKED POTATO (C/U)

Quick and easy

- Slice up leftover baked potatoes and fry in a hot frying pan to make chips.
- Place baked potato skins on a baking tray, sprinkle with oil and bake in a hot oven for about 10-15 mins. Sprinkle with salt and serve like crisps with sour cream dip.

Tip

- To get a really crispy skin to your potato, rub it with a little olive oil and salt before putting it in the oven.

See also

BEEF, LAMB, POTATOES, SWEET CORN.

BANANAS (U)

RECIPES *Basic:* Cake Mix (p.80), Fruit Salad (p.83), Smoothies (p.86). *Individual:* Pancake Fillings (pp.128-30), Banana and Chocolate Digestive Pudding (p.156), Banana Bread (p.158).

Quick and easy

- Slice a banana lengthways and fill with pieces of chocolate. Wrap the banana in foil and bake for about 15 minutes in a medium oven.

Tips

- Bananas emit a gas that ripens fruit so, unless you have unripe fruit, keep bananas separate from the rest of the fruit bowl.
- Bananas that have gone a bit brown are still great for smoothies or some puddings – see Banana and Chocolate Digestive Pudding.
- Some local shops will sell bunches of 'brown' bananas at a cut-down price, so look out for them – there are so many things you can make with them, e.g. Banana Bread.

Can also be used in

Mixed Fruit Cheesecake (p.170).

BEANS (C/U)

See BROAD BEANS, FRENCH BEANS, RUNNER BEANS.

BEEF (C)

RECIPES *Basic:* Curry (p.58), Pasties – Savoury (p.59), Meat Pie (p.62), Shepherd's/Cottage Pie (p.63), Risotto (p.65), Rissoles (p.66), Stir-fry (p.74). *Individual:* Braised Beef with Winter Vegetables (p.94), Chilli Con Carne (p.105).

Quick and easy
- Cold roast beef is almost better than hot! Serve sliced with a baked potato and horseradish sauce.

Tips
- Cold, cooked beef can easily be minced in a food processor or using an old fashioned mincer.
- If you are stripping a joint of beef, if possible leave the meat on the bone and cover until you need it as it prevents the meat from drying out too much.
- Beef dripping adds flavour when used for frying bacon and roasting potatoes. It will keep in the fridge for up to two weeks.

Can also be used in
Salad (pp.68-9), Lamb Pitta Pockets (p.121), Lamb Samosas (p.122), Pork Enchiladas (p.133).

BEER
RECIPES *Basic:* Meat or Shepherd's/Cottage Pie (pp.62-3).

Tip
Keep any flat beer – it's a great addition to stews and pies, adding flavour to the sauce.

BISCUITS
RECIPES *Individual:* Banana and Chocolate Digestive Pudding (p.156), Lemon Meringue Pie (p.167), Mixed Fruit Cheesecake (p.170).

Quick and easy
- Crumbs or old biscuits from the bottom of the biscuit tin can be used as toppings for many puddings, such as yoghurt and fruit or as the base for a cheesecake or banoffi pie.

Can also be used in
Crumble – Fruit (p.82).

BLACKBERRIES (U)
RECIPES *Basic:* Crumble/Pie – Fruit (p.82), Fruit Salad (p.83), Pasties – Sweet (p.84), Stewed Fruit (p.88). *Individual:* Summer Fruits Frozen Yoghurt (p.172), Summer Pudding (p.173).

Tips
- Blackberries can be picked for free out of the hedges towards the end of the summer, early autumn.
- Pick them while they are ripe and then freeze by laying them out on a tray and putting the tray in the freezer. When the fruit has frozen, divide into portions and store in freezer bags.

BLACKCURRANTS (U)
RECIPES *Basic:* Crumble/Pie – Fruit (p.82), Fruit Salad (p.83), Smoothies (p.86), Stewed Fruit (p.88), Fruit Juices (pp.117-9). *Individual:* Mixed Fruit Cheesecake (p.170), Summer Fruits Frozen Yoghurt (p.172), Summer Pudding (p.173).

Tips
- The easiest way to get blackcurrants off their stalks is to use a fork.
See 'Blackberries' for freezing advice.

BLUEBERRIES (U)
RECIPES *Basic:* Crumble/Pie – Fruit (p.82), Fruit Salad (p.83), Smoothies (p.86), Fruit Juices (pp.117-9). *Individual:* Mixed Fruit Cheesecake (p.170), Summer Fruits Frozen Yoghurt (p.172), Summer Pudding (p.173).

Quick and easy
- Blueberries are classified as a 'superfruit' so try some on cereal or muesli in the morning, with a dollop of yoghurt.

BOLOGNAISE SAUCE (C)

RECIPES *Individual:* Baked Potato Fillings (pp.92-3).

Quick and easy

- Heat up and serve with a thick slice of bread and butter.
- Try adding a little chilli powder and perhaps some tinned kidney beans to turn it into a Chilli Con Carne.

BREAD

RECIPES *Basic:* Fish Pie (p.61), Rissoles (p.66). *Individual:* Chicken Crunch (p.102), Fish Cakes (p.110), Ham Loaf with Pineapple (p.113), Roasted Vegetable Bruschetta (p.136), Bread and Butter Pudding (p.160), Summer Pudding (p.173).

Quick and easy

- Bread sauce (delicious with roast chicken or turkey) – bring about 300ml of milk to the boil in a saucepan with some cloves, a small onion and bay leaf.
- Simmer for 20 minutes, remove from the heat and add about 200g stale breadcrumbs (or enough to make a thick sauce).
- Mix well.

Tips

- Make breadcrumbs by processing stale bread in a food processor until all the lumps are removed. Freeze in freezer bags and use when needed.
- Make croutons, to put in salads and soup, by frying cubed, stale bread in oil until brown, or coating in olive oil and baking in a hot oven until brown.
- If bread rolls or pitta seem a little hard, wet the outside with water and stick in a hot oven for about 2 minutes, this will refresh the bread nicely.
- Make bruschetta by slicing up stale French bread, coating both sides in olive oil and baking in a moderate oven for 15 minutes.

- Slice up stale croissants and use them instead of bread for a bread and butter pudding.

Can also be used in

Macaroni Cheese (p.124).

See also

GARLIC, PASTA, SAUSAGES.

BROAD BEANS (C/U)

RECIPES *Basic:* Crumble/Pie – Vegetable (p.57), Curry (p.58), Salad (pp.68-9). *Individual:* Vegetable Stew (p.152).

Quick and easy

- Add cold broad beans to a salad or mix them with mayonnaise and black pepper
- Deep fry them in very hot vegetable oil in a wok or frying pan until they turn a light colour. Drain well and sprinkle with salt. Serve as a nibble.
- Boil them for a minute to soften. Fry some chopped bacon and spring onion, add the beans and black pepper and serve on bruschetta brushed with garlic for a delicious light supper or snack.

Tip

- In general, the smaller the bean the more delicious it is. With big beans, peel skin off for tenderness.

BROCCOLI (C/U)

RECIPES *Basic:* Crumble/Pie – Vegetable (p.57), Curry (p.58), Quiche (p.64), Risotto (p.65), Soup (p.73), Stir-fry (p.74), Vegetable Juices (pp.117-8). *Individual:* Bubble and Squeak (p.95), Butternut Squash Coconut Curry (p.96), Chicken Crunch (p.102), Stuffed Peppers with Rice (p.145), Turkey and Broccoli Hollandaise (p.149), Vegetable and Lentil Bake (p.150), Vegetable Stew (p.152).

Quick and easy

- Roast any 'lonely' broccoli florets in olive oil with pine nuts.

Tips
- Store in the fridge to avoid broccoli turning yellow.
- Avoid overcooking – steaming it is best and retains the goodness.

Can also be used in
Sauce – White (p.70).

BRUSSELS SPROUTS (C/U)

RECIPES *Basic:* Crumble/Pie – Vegetable (p.57). *Individual:* Bubble and Squeak (p.95).

Quick and easy
- Cold Brussels sprouts can be tossed in a saucepan with hot butter, almonds and black pepper or served cold with some cold turkey and cranberry sauce.

Tip
- Brussels sprouts are cheapest in early winter when they are in season.

Can also be used in
Chutney (p.56), Soup (p.73).

See also
NUTS.

BULGUR WHEAT (C)

Quick and easy
- Mix bulgur wheat with leftover roasted vegetables or cooked prawns or the remains of a stir-fry.
- Make a Lebanese salad with bulgur wheat and grilled halloumi, toasted pine nuts, parsley and chopped tomatoes.

Tip
- Use bulgur wheat as a quick alternative to rice.

Can also be used in
Stuffed Peppers with Rice (p.145).

See also
COUSCOUS, STOCK.

BURGERS (C)

Quick and easy
- Crumble up cold leftover burgers and add them to a pasta sauce or shepherd's pie or use as an addition to a pizza topping.

Can also be used in
Meat Pie (p.62), Shepherd's/Cottage Pie (p.63), Sauce – Tomato (p.72).

CABBAGE (GREEN) (C/U)

RECIPES *Basic:* Crumble/Pie – Vegetable (p.57), Soup (p.73), Stir-fry (p.74), Vegetable Juices (pp.117-8). *Individual:* Bubble and Squeak (p.95), Chicken Spring Rolls (p.104).

Quick and easy
- Cut up cooked cabbage very fine and add to fish cakes.
- Shred raw cabbage finely and add to salad or coleslaw.

CABBAGE (RED) (C/U)

RECIPES *Basic:* Chutney (p.56), Crumble/Pie – Vegetable (p.57), Vegetable Juices (pp.117-8).

Quick and easy
- Reheat cooked leftover red cabbage and add raisins, chopped apple and nutmeg.
- Raw red cabbage can be shredded finely and added to salad or coleslaw.

Can also be used in
Stir-fry (p.74), Bubble and Squeak (p.95).

CARROTS: (C/U)

RECIPES *Basic:* Crumble/Pie – Vegetable (p.57), Curry (p.58), Pasties – Savoury (p.59), Chicken Pie (p.60), Fish Pie (p.61), Meat Pie (p.62) and Shepherd's/Cottage Pie (p.63), Risotto (p.65),

Rissoles (p.66), Roasted Vegetables (p.67), Soup (p.73), Stir-fry (p.74), Stock (pp.75-8), Vegetable Juices (pp.117-8). *Individual:* Braised Beef with Winter Vegetables (p.94), Butternut Squash Coconut Curry (p.96), Carrot and Cumin Soup (p.98), Chicken Spring Rolls (p.104), Ham Loaf with Pineapple (p.113), Lamb Samosas (p.122), Pottage (p.134), Vegetable and Lentil Bake (p.150), Vegetable Stew (p.152).

Quick and easy

- Use up any raw carrots by slicing them lengthways and eating them with dips or houmous for a tasty and nutritious snack.
- Add cooked carrots to stews and pies.
- Blend raw carrot to make carrot juice.
- Grate carrot onto salad for extra colour and flavour.

Can also be used in

Salad (pp.68-9), Sauce – Tomato (p.72).

See also

ORANGES.

CAULIFLOWER (C/U)

RECIPES *Basic:* Chutney (p.56), Crumble/Pie – Vegetable (p.57), Curry (p.58), Stir-fry (p.74). *Individual:* Butternut Squash Coconut Curry (p.96), Vegetable Stew (p.152).

Quick and easy

- Steamed cauliflower covered in cheese sauce makes an easy meal. Add chopped up bacon or ham, cooked mushrooms or peas or a teaspoon of grainy mustard to the sauce.
- Add cooked cauliflower to a curry.
- Use raw cauliflower heads to dip into houmous, taramasalata or sour cream dip.

Tip

- Wherever possible, steam your vegetables instead to retain the goodness – up to 90% of the goodness can be lost by boiling vegetables in water.

Can also be used in

Pasties – Savoury (p.59), Lamb Samosas (p.122).

CELERY (U)

RECIPES *Basic:* Chutney (p.56), Crumble (or Pie) – Vegetable, Curry (p.58), Meat Pie (p.62), Salad (pp.68-9), Soup (p.73), Stock (pp.75-8). *Individual:* Carrot and Cumin Soup (p.98), Vegetable Juices (pp.117-8), Leek and Potato Soup (p.123), Spicy Sausage Stew (p.144), Vegetable Stew (p.152).

Quick and easy

- Slice lengthways and eat with a dip.
- Use the last celery stick to make juice – really tasty mixed with carrot juice.

Tips

- Celery lasts much longer if it is kept in the fridge.
- Don't waste celery leaves – add finely chopped leaves to a salad.

Can also be used in

Stir-fry (p.74).

See also

MAYONNAISE.

CEREAL

RECIPES *Individual:* Chocolate Crispy Cakes (p.162).

Tips

- Always fold down the top of the plastic inner packaging when storing cereal as it will keep fresh longer.
- Soft cornflakes can sometimes be made crispy again by laying them out on a baking sheet and cooking them in a hot oven for about 3 minutes.

See also

FRUIT (STEWED), GRAPES, RHUBARB.

CHEESE

RECIPES *Basic:* Pasties – Savoury (p.59), Quiche (p.64), Salad (pp.68-9), Sauce (p.70), Soup (p.73). *Individual:* Baked Potato Fillings (pp.92-3), Cheese Soufflé (p.99), Cheesy Chicken Breasts (p.100), Cheesy Leeks and Ham (p.101), Chicken Crunch (p.102), Macaroni Cheese (p.124), Pancake Fillings (pp.128-30), Pork Enchiladas (p.133), Pottage (p.134), Salad Dressings (pp.138-9), Spanish Omelette (p.142), Stuffed Peppers with Rice (p.145), Vegetable and Lentil Bake (p.150), Scones (p.171).

Quick and easy

- Cheese on toast – try spreading mustard on the toast before putting the cheese on or add a slice of ham underneath the cheese.
- Goat's cheese is great to use in sandwiches as it spreads very well.

Tips

- Store in airtight container or greaseproof paper.
- If cheese gets a bit hard or mouldy at the end, don't worry, just cut it off. Hard bits can still be grated and used in a sauce.

Can also be used in

Chicken Pie (p.60) or Fish Pie (p.61).

See also

CAULIFLOWER, HAM, LEEKS, PANCAKES, PASTA, POTATOES, SPINACH, TUNA.

CHERRIES (U)

RECIPES *Basic:* Fruit Salad (p.83). *Individual:* Mixed Fruit Cheesecake (p.170).

Quick and easy

- If you only have a few cherries left, halve them, take out the stones and add them to yoghurt or on top of muesli.

Tip

- Store cherries in the fridge as they are an expensive fruit – they will keep longer.

CHICKEN (C)

RECIPES *Basic:* Curry (p.58), Chicken/Turkey Pie (p.60), Quiche (p.64), Risotto (p.65), Rissoles (p.66), Salad (pp.68-9), Sauce (pp.70-2), Soup (p.73), Stir-fry (p.74), Stock (p.75). *Individual:* Baked Potato Fillings (p.92-3), Butternut Squash Coconut Curry (p.96), Cheesy Chicken Breasts (p.100), Chicken Crunch (p.102), Chicken Spring Rolls (p.104), Coronation Turkey (p.107), Pancake Fillings (pp.128-30).

Quick and easy

- Use chicken livers (if they come with the chicken) to make stock for gravy by simmering them in water with half an onion and salt and pepper, for about an hour.
- Make hot chicken, bacon and mayonnaise paninis for a filling lunch.

Tips

- When stripping the meat from a roast chicken carcass, it is much easier to do it when the meat is still warm.
- Keep the stripped meat in a cool place and well covered to prevent it drying out.

Can also be used in

Chinese Pork with Water Chestnuts (p.106), Lamb Pitta Pockets (p.121), Lamb Samosas (p.122), Macaroni Cheese (p.124), Pork Enchiladas (p.133).

See also

CHILLIES, MAYONNAISE, PESTO, SWEET CORN, YOGHURT.

CHICK PEAS (TINNED)

RECIPES *Basic:* Soup (p.73). *Individual:* Instant Onion and Bean Stew (p.116).

Quick and easy

- Houmous – combine a tin of chick peas with 2 tablespoons of tahini, juice of one lemon, 2 cloves of garlic and a little water. Use raw vegetables cut into strips to dip into it.

Tip

Tinned chick peas are great for bulking out a soup or stew.

Can also be used in

Meat Pie (p.62), Salad (pp.68-9).

CHILLIES (U)

RECIPES *Individual:* Butternut Squash Coconut Curry (p.96), Chicken Spring Rolls (p.104), Chilli Con Carne (p.105), Guacamole (p.112), Harissa Sauce (p.114), Lamb Samosas (p.122), Mixed Nut and Tofu Roast (p.126), Sweet Potato and Prawn Cakes (p.146).

Quick and easy

- Try marinating meat or chicken in chopped chillies with lime or lemon juice for at least an hour before cooking.

Tip

- Make sure you wash your hands straight after cutting chillies and do not rub your eyes!

Can also be used in

Soup (p.73), Stir-fry (p.74), Cheesy Chicken Breasts (p.100), Ratatouille (p.135).

CHOCOLATE (U)

RECIPES *Individual:* Pancake Fillings (pp.128-30), Chocolate Crispy Cakes (p.162), Tiramisu Ice Cream (p.174).

Quick and easy

- Melt any leftover chocolate in a bowl over a saucepan of boiling water and pour over ice cream
- Grate it over sweet puddings to add a little cheer.

Tip

- Always store in an airtight container.

Can also be used in

Cake Mix (p.80), Banana Bread (p.158), Blueberry Muffins (p.159), Bread and Butter Pudding (p.160), Flapjacks (p.168), Mixed Fruit Cheesecake (p.170).

See also

BANANAS, COFFEE.

CHORIZO (C)

RECIPES *Individual:* Spicy Sausage Stew (p.144).

Quick and easy

- Fry up chorizo slices and add to a tomato pasta sauce.
- Add to any meat casseroles or lentil stew.

Tip

- It's much cheaper to buy a whole chorizo sausage rather than the slices sold in supermarkets or delicatessens.

Can also be used in

Salad (pp.68-9), Courgette and Pasta Bake (p.108), Spanish Omelette (p.142), Vegetable and Lentil Bake (p.150).

CHRISTMAS PUDDING (C)

RECIPES *Individual:* Christmas Pudding Crème Brulée (p.164).

Quick and easy

- Slice the Christmas pudding and fry in a little butter. Serve with cream or brandy butter.
- Mix the Christmas pudding in with some slightly softened vanilla ice cream and a drop or two of brandy for a delicious pudding.

Tip

- If kept in an airtight container, Christmas pudding will keep for several months.

COFFEE (C)

RECIPES *Individual:* Iced Coffee (p.166), Tiramisu Ice Cream (p.174).

Quick and easy

- Add a little strong cold coffee to a chocolate sauce to pour over ice cream or a chocolate sponge. (Not advisable for children).

C

A-Z of Leftovers

COURGETTES (C/U)

RECIPES *Basic:* Crumble/Pie – Vegetable (p.57), Roasted Vegetables (p.67), Stir-fry (p.74).
Individual: Courgette and Pasta Bake (p.108), Ratatouille (p.135), Roasted Vegetable Bruschetta (p.136), Roast Vegetable Kebabs with Halloumi (p.151), Vegetable Stew (p.152).

Quick and easy

- Slice and fry raw courgettes in some butter and garlic and serve with lots of black pepper.
- Add finely sliced raw courgette to salads.

Can also be used in
Lamb Pitta Pockets (p.121).

See also
COUSCOUS, LEMONS.

COUSCOUS (C)

Quick and easy

- Try using leftover couscous instead of rice, served with cold meats or roasted vegetables.
- Make a quick salad with couscous and chopped tomatoes, cucumber, raw red onion and courgettes with a slug of olive oil and lemon juice.
- Serve with barbecued kebabs in the summer.

Tip

- Store in an airtight container to prevent leftover couscous from drying out.

Can also be used in
Salad (pp.68-9), Harissa with Prawns and Couscous (p.115), Stuffed Peppers with Rice (p.145).

See also
BULGUR WHEAT, DRIED FRUIT.

CREAM

RECIPES *Basic:* Curry (p.58), Quiche (p.64), Sauce – White (p.70), Soup (p.73). *Individual:* Coronation Turkey (p.107), Courgette and Pasta Bake (p.108), Green Pea Soup (p.111), Leek and Potato Soup (p.123), Pancake Fillings (pp.128-30), Bread and Butter Pudding (p.160), Christmas Pudding Crème Brulée (p.164), Iced Coffee (p.166), Tiramisu Ice Cream (p.174).

Quick and easy

- Add a dollop of cream to stews or casseroles to thicken sauces.

Can also be used in
Soup (p.73), Cake Mix (p.80), Banana and Chocolate Digestive Pudding (p.156), Meringues (p.169).

See also
BAKED POTATOES, CHICKEN, CHRISTMAS PUDDING, FROMAGE FRAIS, PEACHES, PIE.

CRÈME FRAÎCHE

RECIPES *Individual:* Baked Potato Fillings (pp.92-3).

Quick and easy

- If you have a little bit of crème fraîche left in the pot, add a dollop on top of tomato-based pasta dishes or fruit puddings.
- Fry, in a little olive oil, a red onion with some chopped bacon and mushrooms. Take off the heat and add two tablespoons of crème fraîche, mix in well and serve with pasta.

Can also be used in
Curry (p.58).

See also
ONIONS (RED).

CRISPS

RECIPES *Individual:* Chicken Crunch (p.102), Macaroni Cheese (p.124).

Quick and easy

- Crunch up stale crisps and scatter on top of fish pie with some grated cheese.

CUCUMBER (U)

RECIPES *Basic:* Salad (pp.68-9), Soup (p.73). *Individual:* Tsatsiki (p.148).

Quick and easy

- Cut cucumbers into fingers and dip into houmous, taramasalata or other flavoured dips.
- Mix finely sliced cucumber with sour cream and chives and serve with salmon fillets.

Tip

- Half a leftover cucumber can be sliced and put in a jar of spiced vinegar – it will keep for two months.

See also
COUSCOUS, KIDNEY BEANS, ONIONS, RICE.

CURRY (C)

RECIPES *Basic:* Curry (p.58).

Quick and easy

- Don't throw away the remains of a takeaway curry. It can easily be heated up although meat-based curries should not be kept for more than two days after purchase.
- Vegetable curries can be added to a stir-fry.

CUSTARD

Quick and easy

- Custard is one of life's little treats and can easily be reheated if leftover. Try warming it up and adding a chopped up banana.

See also
PIE.

DATES

RECIPES *Individual:* Christmas Date Biscuits (p.163).

Quick and easy

- Bacon-wrapped dates – wrap half a rasher of streaky bacon around each pitted date and secure with a toothpick. Bake in a moderate oven for 15 minutes until the bacon is crisp. Serve as a 'nibble'.

DRIED FRUIT

RECIPES *Basic:* Chutney (p.56), Curry (p.58), Salad (pp.68-9). *Individual:* Baked Potato Fillings (pp.92-3), Coronation Turkey (p.107), Pancake Fillings (pp.128-30), Bread and Butter Pudding (p.160), Scones (p.171).

Quick and easy

- Sprinkle chopped dried fruit on cereal or in porridge.
- Lovely just as a quick energy-giving snack – particularly good in school/work packed lunches
- Add to a rice salad or couscous/bulgur wheat salad.

Tip

- It's always good to have a variety of dried fruits in the store cupboard as they are a useful addition to a number of dishes e.g. rice or couscous/bulgur wheat salad, curries.

See also
CHICKEN, PEARS.

EGGS

RECIPES *Basic:* **Fish Pie (p.61), Quiche (p.64), Cake Mix (p.80).** *Individual:* **Cheese Soufflé (p.99), Chinese Pork with Water Chestnuts (p.106), Eggs over Peppers and Tomatoes (p.109), Ham Loaf with Pineapple (p.113), Kedgeree (p.120), Mayonnaise (p.125), Mixed Nut and Tofu Roast (p.126), Spanish Omelette (p.142), Banana Bread (p.158), Blueberry Muffins (p.159), Bread and Butter Pudding (p.160), Christmas Pudding Crème Brulée (p.164), Lemon Meringue Pie (p.167), Meringues (p.169), Mixed Fruit Cheesecake (p.170), Tiramisu Ice Cream (p.174).**

Quick and easy

· Use leftover scrambled egg to make an egg and mayonnaise sandwich.

· Quick omelette – whisk two eggs in a bowl, season with salt and pepper, and transfer to a non-stick frying pan and cook for about 7 minutes over a medium heat, until all the egg has set. Add grated cheese, tomato, cooked mushrooms, ham or bacon whilst the egg is still runny.

Tip

· To test for freshness, put egg in a bowl of water. A fresh egg will sink to the bottom and lie on its side. Older eggs will stand up on one end; really old eggs will float and should be discarded.

Can also be used in
Salad (pp.68-9), Sauce – White (p.70).

See also
SPINACH.

FENNEL

RECIPES *Individual:* **Tomato and Fennel Gazpacho (p.147).**

Quick and easy

· Fry sliced up fennel in butter for 5 minutes. Add some single cream and crème fraîche and warm through. Transfer to an oven dish and sprinkle Parmesan over the top. Bake in a reasonably hot oven for about 25-30 minutes until brown on top.

Tip

· Fennel dries out quickly so it should be stored in the fridge and used within 3-4 days.

FISH (C)

RECIPES *Basic:* **Fish Pie (p.61), Quiche (p.64), Stock (p.77).** *Individual:* **Fish Cakes (p.110), Kedgeree (p.120).**

Quick and easy

· Oily fish such as pilchards, sardines and anchovies can be added to a salad, or the top of a pizza or mushed up on toast.

Tip

· Fish will only stay fresh in the fridge for about 3-4 days so good menu planning is needed.

Can also be used in
Salad (pp.68-9), Soup (p.73).

FRENCH (GREEN) BEANS (C/U)

RECIPES *Basic:* **Chutney (p.56), Risotto (p.65), Salad (pp.68-9), Stir-fry (p.74), Vegetable Juices (pp.117-8).**

Quick and easy

· Cold French beans are delicious just tossed in a little vinaigrette and lots of black pepper.

Can also be used in
Spanish Omelette (p.142).

See also
POTATOES.

FROMAGE FRAIS

Quick and easy
- If you have a little bit left in the bottom of the pot, this is delicious as a substitute for cream on puddings and fruit.

See also
HAM.

FRUIT (STEWED)

Quick and easy
- Leftover stewed fruit is delicious on top of cereal or muesli or mixed with some natural yoghurt and brown sugar.

See also
Individual fruit names, e.g. APPLE.

GAMMON (C)

See HAM.

GARLIC

RECIPES *Basic:* Chutney (p.56), Curry (p.58), Pasties – Savoury (p.59), Chicken/Turkey Pie (p.60), Meat Pie (p.62), Shepherd's/Cottage Pie (p.63), Risotto (p.65), Rissoles (p.66), Roasted Vegetables (p.67), Salad (pp.68-9), Sauce (pp.71-2), Soup (p.73). *Individual:* Braised Beef with Winter Vegetables (p.94), Butternut Squash Coconut Curry (p.96), Carrot and Cumin Soup (p.98), Chicken Liver and Wild Mushroom Pâté (p.103), Chicken Spring Rolls (p.104), Chilli Con Carne (p.105), Chinese Pork with Water Chestnuts (p.106), Courgette and Pasta Bake (p.108), Guacamole (p.112), Harissa Sauce (p.114), Lamb Samosas (p.122), Mayonnaise (p.125), Mixed Nut and Tofu Roast (p.126), Ratatouille (p.135), Roasted Vegetable Bruschetta (p.136), Salad Dressings (pp.138-9), Spicy Sausage Stew (p.144), Stuffed Peppers with Rice (p.145), Sweet Potato and Prawn Cakes (p.146), Tomato and Fennel Gazpacho (p.147), Tsatsiki (p.148), Vegetable and Lentil Bake (p.150), Vegetable Stew (p.152).

Quick and easy
- For delicious garlic bread, crush a clove of garlic, add a tablespoon of soft butter and mix up well. Slice a loaf of French bread and butter the slices with the garlic and butter mixture. Put the loaf together again, wrap in aluminium foil and bake in a moderate oven for 10 minutes.
- For bruschetta, take a slice of stale French bread, toast both sides and rub one side with a garlic clove. Cover with whatever topping you like.

See also
AUBERGINES, BROAD BEANS, CHICK PEAS, COURGETTES, LENTILS, MUSHROOMS.

GRAPEFRUIT (U)

RECIPES *Basic:* Fruit Salad (p.83), Fruit Juices (pp.117-9).

Quick and easy
- Cut grapefruit in half and sprinkle each half with a dash of sherry and soft brown or muscovado sugar. Pop under a hot grill for 5 minutes until the sugar melts.

Tip
- Even if grapefruit is a bit crinkled or too soft, the zest can be used to add flavour to fruit puddings.

GRAPES (U)

RECIPES *Basic:* Fruit Salad (p.83), Fruit Juices (pp.117-9).

Quick and easy

- Chop up the grapes into some natural or flavoured yoghurt and sprinkle some muesli or crunchy cereal on top for a quick pudding. A drizzle of honey or maple syrup on top makes it even more delicious.
- Add to a curry, rice salad or risotto at the last minute for extra flavour.

Can also be used in
Curry (p.58), Risotto (p.65), Baked Potato Fillings (pp.92-3).

See also
CHICKEN.

GRAVY

RECIPES *Basic:* Chicken/Turkey Pie (p.60), Meat Pie (p.62), Shepherd's/Cottage Pie (p.63).

Tip

- Don't throw away leftover gravy, it is ideal to add flavour to a savoury pie or soup.

See also
PIE.

GREENS (C)

RECIPES *Individual:* Bubble and Squeak (p.95).

Quick and easy

- Cooked greens can be heated up by tossing them in hot melted butter in a saucepan for a couple of minutes. Add chopped ham or chopped tomatoes.

HAM (C)

RECIPES *Basic:* Quiche (p.64). *Individual:* Baked Potato Fillings (pp.92-3), Cheesy Leeks and Ham (p.101), Ham Loaf with Pineapple (p.113).

Quick and easy

- Chop ham and add it to any salad or mix it with cheese and mayonnaise or fromage frais to have on top of a baked potato.

Can also be used in
Chicken pie (p.60) or Meat Pie (p.62), Salad (pp.68-9), Sauce – white (p.70), Sauce – tomato (p.72), Courgette and Pasta Bake (p.108), Macaroni Cheese (p.124), Spanish Omelette (p.142), Risotto (p.65), Stuffed Peppers with Rice (p.145), Vegetable and Lentil Bake (p.150).

See also
CAULIFLOWER, EGGS, GREENS.

ICE CREAM

RECIPES *Basic:* Smoothies (p.86).

Quick and easy

- If your ice cream has melted, try pouring it over fruit salad or other sweet puddings.

Tip

- Don't let ice cream melt – refreezing it after it has melted is very difficult as the ingredients separate and the resulting ice cream becomes crystallised.

JUICES

RECIPES *Basic:* Fruit Salad (p.83).

Quick and easy

- Add leftover juice to some chopped fruit to make a fruit salad or use it on your cereal instead of milk.

KIDNEY BEANS (TINNED)

RECIPES *Basic:* Salad (pp.68-9). *Individual:* Chilli Con Carne (p.105).

Quick and easy

- Mix cooked beans with some cubed cucumber, tomato and red onion and add a little vinaigrette for a really quick bean salad.

Tip

- Add tinned kidney beans to a stew to bulk it out if you are a bit short of meat.

See also
BOLOGNAISE SAUCE.

LAMB (C)

RECIPES *Basic:* Curry (p.58), Pasties – Savoury (p.59), Meat or Shepherd's/Cottage Pie (pp.62-3), Risotto (p.65), Rissoles (p.66), Stir-fry (p.74), Stock (p.76). *Individual:* Lamb Pitta Pockets (p.121), Lamb Samosas (p.122).

Quick and easy

· Cold, cooked lamb is delicious served with a baked potato and green salad.
· Mix diced cooked lamb with fried onions and cooked green beans and cover in a heated-up tomato sauce.

Tip

· Cooked lamb should be cooled quickly and stored in the fridge or a cool place. Keep covered in aluminium foil to stop the meat from drying out.

Can also be used in

Chinese Pork with Water Chestnuts (p.106).

LEEKS (C/U)

RECIPES *Basic:* Crumble/Pie – Vegetable (p.57), Curry (p.58), Pasties – Savoury (p.59), Chicken/Turkey Pie (p.60), Meat Pie (p.62), Shepherd's/Cottage Pie (p.63), Roasted Vegetables (p.67), Soup (p.73), Stir-fry (p.74). *Individual:* Braised Beef with Winter Vegetables (p.94), Cheesy Leeks and Ham (p.101), Chicken Crunch (p.102), Ham Loaf with Pineapple (p.113), Leek and Potato Soup (p.123), Vegetable and Lentil Bake (p.150), Vegetable Stew (p.152).

Quick and easy

· Cooked leeks can be reheated by tossing in hot melted butter in a saucepan.
· Pour a cheese sauce over cooked leeks and perhaps chopped crispy bacon.

Tip

· Even if the outer layers of the leek have dried out, just peel them off – the inner layers may still be fresh.

Can also be used in

Chicken Pie (p.60) or Meat Pie (p.62), Quiche (p.64), Risotto (p.65), Rissoles (p.66), Sauce (pp.70-2), Fish Cakes (p.110), Lamb Pitta Pockets (p.121), Spanish Omelette (p.142).

LEMONS

RECIPES *Basic:* Risotto (p.65), Stock (p.77), Crumble/Pie–Fruit (p.82), Fruit Salad (p.83), Smoothies (p.86), Stewed Fruit (p.88), Fruit Juices (pp.117-9). *Individual:* Chicken Crunch (p.102), Coronation Turkey (p.107), Guacamole (p.112), Mayonnaise (p.125), Salad Dressings (pp.138-9), Tomato and Fennel Gazpacho (p.147), Turkey and Broccoli Hollandaise (p.149), Vegetable and Lentil Bake (p.150), Banana and Chocolate Digestive Pudding (p.156), Bread and Butter Pudding (p.160), Lemon Meringue Pie (p.167), Treacle Tart (p.176).

Quick and easy

· Squeeze the juice of one lemon into a glass and add fizzy water and maybe a teaspoon of sugar for a really refreshing drink in summer.
· Grate the zest over cooked courgettes.
· Slice lemons and then freeze the slices in freezer bags – ideal to add to drinks.
· Squeeze juice into sauces for flavour.

Tip

· Lemon juice is fantastic for preventing cut vegetables and fruit from discolouring.

Can also be used in

Stir-fry (p.74), Cake Mix (p.80), Fish Cakes (p.110), Mixed Fruit Cheesecake (p.170).

LENTILS

RECIPES *Individual:* Vegetable and Lentil Bake (p.150), Vegetable Stew (p.152).

Quick and easy

- Quick tomato and lentil soup – fry a chopped onion and some garlic, add a tin of chopped tomatoes, some stock and red lentils. Bring to the boil and simmer for 15 minutes with some mixed herbs and black pepper. Try adding a dollop of pesto on top when you serve.

Can also be used in

Pasties – Savoury (p.59), Meat Pie (p.62), Soup (p.73).

LIVER (C)

RECIPE *Individual:* Chicken Liver and Wild Mushroom Pâté (p.103).

Quick and easy

- Thinly slice cooked liver and add to a tomato sauce. Serve with pasta.

Tip

- Keep cooked liver well covered as it has a tendency to dry out very quickly.

MANGE TOUT (C/U)

RECIPES *Basic:* Stir-fry (p.74).

Quick and easy

- Add leftover raw or cooked mange tout to a green salad.

Can also be used in

Salad (pp.68-9).

MAYONNAISE

RECIPES *Basic:* Salad (pp.68-9). *Individual:* Baked Potatoes (pp.92-3), Chicken Crunch (p.102), Coronation Turkey (p.107), Salad Dressings (pp.139-40).

Quick and easy

- Mix with tuna and sweet corn for a sandwich or to use with pasta.
- Mix with crème fraîche and chopped spring onion to make a quick salad dressing for a rice or celery salad.

Tip

- If you want to make a sandwich but there's only a tiny bit of mayonnaise left in a big jar, put the sandwich ingredient in the jar (e.g. tuna, tomatoes, chicken) and shake it around to coat the ingredients in the mayonnaise.

See also

BROAD BEANS, CHICKEN, EGGS, HAM, PASTA, PRAWNS, SWEET CORN, TUNA, YOGHURT.

MEAT (C)

See BEEF, LAMB, PORK.

MELON (U)

RECIPES *Basic:* Fruit Salad (p.83), Fruit Juices (pp.117-9).

Quick and easy

- Add chopped melon pieces to a green or fruit salad.

Tip

- If you have half a melon left over, chop it into pieces and store them in an airtight container.

MILK

RECIPES *Basic:* Pasties – Savoury (p.59), Chicken/Turkey Pie (p.60), Fish Pie (p.61), Quiche (p.64), Sauce – White (p.70), Pasties – Sweet (p.84). *Individual:* Butternut Squash Coconut Curry (p.96), Cheese Soufflé (p.99), Cheesy Leeks and Ham (p.101), Chicken Crunch (p.102), Green Pea Soup (p.111), Ham Loaf with Pineapple (p.113), Kedgeree (p.120), Macaroni Cheese (p.124), Spanish Omelette (p.142), Banana and Yoghurt Scotch Pancakes (p.157), Banana Bread (p.158), Bread and Butter Pudding (p.160), Iced Coffee (p.166), Scones (p.171).

Tip
- Milk can be frozen but don't leave in the freezer for more than a month or the milk may separate when it is thawed out.
- The last drops of milk in a carton can be used to brush over pastry on pies to make the pastry glossy when it cooks.
- Slight 'off' milk is ideal for scones.

MUSHROOMS (C/U)

RECIPES *Basic:* Curry (p.58), Pasties – Savoury (p.59), Chicken/Turkey Pie (p.60), Meat or Shepherd's/ Cottage Pie (pp.62-3), Quiche (p.64), Risotto (p.65), Sauce (pp.70-2), Stir-fry (p.74), Stock (pp.75-8). *Individual:* Baked Potato Fillings (pp.92-3), Chicken Liver and Wild Mushroom Pâté (p.103), Chicken Spring Rolls (p.104), Chinese Pork with Water Chestnuts (p.106), Courgette and Pasta Bake (p.108), Mixed Nut and Tofu Roast (p.126), Pancake Fillings (pp.128-30), Stuffed Peppers with Rice (p.145), Roasted Vegetable and Halloumi Kebabs (p.151), Vegetable Stew (p.152).

Quick and easy
- Fry sliced mushrooms in butter with a crushed clove of garlic. When soft serve on hot buttered toast with cracked black pepper and parsley (optional).

Tip
- Add any leftover, sliced, raw mushrooms to the top of a pizza.
- Wrinkly mushrooms are fine added to a sauce or added to a stew or casserole.
- Mushrooms will last longer in the fridge.

Can also be used in
Salad (pp.68-9), Soup (p.73).

See also
CAULIFLOWER, CRÈME FRAÎCHE, EGGS, ONIONS (RED).

NUTS

RECIPES *Basic:* Rissoles (p.66), Salad (pp.68-9), Stir-fry (p.74). *Individual:* Mixed Nut and Tofu Roast (p.126), Vegetable and Lentil Bake (p.150), Banana Bread (p.158).

Quick and easy
- Crushed nuts are ideal for sprinkling on top of cereal, yoghurt or fruit puddings.
- Roast pine nuts in a hot oven for 5 minutes and sprinkle on top of a Caesar salad or on pesto with pasta.
- Add walnuts or pecan nuts to muffins or brownies.
- Try adding walnuts to green beans tossed in butter, or chestnuts to Brussels sprouts for extra protein and taste.

Tip
- Beware of the possibility of nuts or nut oil as a 'hidden' ingredient if you are feeding someone who may have a nut allergy.
- Keep nuts in an airtight container and they will last for months.

Can also be used in
Cake Mix (p.80).

See also
BROCCOLI, BULGUR WHEAT, RUNNER BEANS, YOGHURT.

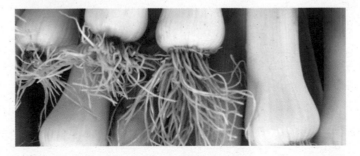

ONIONS (WHITE) (C/U)

RECIPES *Basic:* Chutney (p.56), Crumble (or Pie) – Vegetable (p.57), Pasties – Savoury (p.59), Chicken/Turkey Pie (p.60), Meat Pie (p.62), Shepherd's/Cottage Pie (p.63), Quiche (p.64), Risotto (p.65), Roasted Vegetables (p.67), Salad (pp.68-9), Soup (p.73), Stock (pp.75-8). *Individual:* Braised Beef with Winter Vegetables (p.94), Bubble and Squeak (p.95), Chilli Con Carne (p.105), Instant Onion and Bean Stew (p.116), Kedgeree (p.120), Lamb Samosas (p.122), Pottage (p.134), Ratatouille (p.135), Roasted Vegetable Bruschetta (p.136), Spicy Sausage Stew (p.144), Stuffed Peppers with Rice (p.145), Turkey and Broccoli Hollandaise (p.149), Vegetable and Lentil Bake (p.150), Vegetable Stew (p.152).

Quick and easy
- If you have half an onion left over in the vegetable rack, slice it up and roast it with sausages in the oven. The juice from the sausages will add real substance to the onions.
- Serve leftover cooked onion with cold meat and chutney.

Tip
- Onions must be stored in a cool, dry place. If you've got space, try hanging them in a string bag.

See also
LAMB, POTATOES.

ONIONS (RED) (C/U)

RECIPES *Basic:* Roasted Vegetables (p.67). *Individual:* Caramelised Onion and Tomato Tart (p.97), Roasted Vegetable and Halloumi Kebabs (p.151).

Quick and easy
- For really quick pasta sauce, fry chopped red onion, bacon and mushrooms in a little oil. When they are cooked, add some crème fraîche, warm through and serve on your favourite pasta with lots of black pepper.

See also
ORANGES.

ORANGES (U)

RECIPES *Basic:* Fruit Salad (p.83), Fruit Juices (pp.117-9). *Individual:* Caramelised Oranges (p.161).

Quick and easy
- Make a quick salsa dressing by chopping up an orange into small pieces with a chopped tomato, finely chopped red onion, a slug of olive oil and a tablespoon of pickle or chutney.
- Moroccan salad – peel and dice an orange and place in a bowl with 3 tablespoons of olive oil, 2 tablespoons white wine vinegar, some toasted cumin seeds (toasted for about 10 minutes in the oven) and cubed goat's cheese, beetroot and grated raw carrots.

Tip
- Even when an orange seems to be soft or wrinkly, very often the juice will still be delicious so squeeze the orange juice and freeze it if you're not using it straight away.

Can also be used in
Mixed Fruit Cheesecake (p.170).

PANCAKES (C)

RECIPES *Individual:* Pancake Fillings (pp.128-30).

Quick and easy
- Pancakes can be stuffed with sweet or savoury fillings and are good for using up leftovers, e.g. cooked spinach and cheese sauce, or chopped banana with maple syrup and lemon juice.

Tips
- If you have made too many pancakes, the leftovers can be frozen individually between layers of grease-proof paper and all wrapped in aluminium foil.
- To reheat leftover pancakes, stack the pancakes

on an ovenproof dish, cover with foil and heat in a moderate oven for 10 minutes, or stack and and microwave on high for 30 seconds max.

PARSNIPS (C/U)

RECIPES *Basic:* Crumble/Pie – Vegetable (p.57), Meat Pie (p.62), Roasted Vegetables (p.67), Soup (p.73), Stock (pp.75-8). *Individual:* Braised Beef with Winter Vegetables (p.94), Pottage (p.134), Vegetable Stew (p.152).

Quick and easy
· Leftover roast parsnips are delicious if sliced and fried as an alternative to chips.

Tip
· Parsnips are cheapest in season, from late autumn through to winter.

Can also be used in
Stir-fry (p.74).

PASTA (C)

RECIPES *Basic:* Salad (pp.68-9). *Individual:* Courgette and Pasta Bake (p.108), Macaroni Cheese (p.124).

Quick and easy
· Mix cold pasta with mayonnaise, tinned tuna and tinned sweet corn for a quick snack.
· Simple pasta bake – pour a tin of chopped tomatoes over cooked pasta in an ovenproof dish and perhaps a tin of sweet corn. Add some mixed herbs and sprinkle grated cheese/ breadcrumbs/chopped nuts and bake in a moderate oven for 20 minutes.

See also
CRÈME FRAÎCHE, LIVER, NUTS, ONIONS (RED), PESTO.

PEACHES (U)

RECIPES *Basic:* Cake Mix (p.80), Crumble/Pie – Fruit (p.82), Fruit Salad (p.83), Pasties – Sweet (p.84), Smoothies (p.86), Stewed Fruit (p.88), Fruit Juices (pp.117-9). *Individual:* Baked Apples and Pears (p.155), Grilled Peaches with Cinnamon and Rum Sauce (p.165).

Quick and easy
· If peaches are a little soft, slice them up, coat slices in sugar and place under a hot grill for 5-7 minutes. Serve with cream or crème fraîche.

Tip
· Peaches often ripen and then go off very quickly. Try keeping them in the fridge and only bringing them out into the fruit bowl a few days before they are going to be eaten.

PEARS (U)

RECIPES *Basic:* Chutney (p.56), Crumble/Pie – Fruit (p.82), Fruit Salad (p.83), Pasties – Sweet (p.84), Smoothies (p.86), Stewed Fruit (p.88). *Individual:* Apple and Cinnamon Fritters (p.154), Baked Apples and Pears (p.155).

Quick and easy
· Core the pears and stuff with dried fruit. Bake in the oven for about 20-25 minutes, sitting the pears in shallow water to prevent them from drying out. You can also use this recipe for slightly soft apples.

PEAS (C/U)

RECIPES *Basic:* Crumble/Pie – Vegetable (p.57), Curry (p.58), Pasties – Savoury (p.59), Chicken/Turkey Pie (p.60), Fish Pie (p.61), Meat Pie (p.62), Shepherd's/Cottage Pie (p.63), Quiche (p.64), Risotto (p.65), Rissoles (p.66), Salad (pp.68-9), Soup (p.73). *Individual:* Chicken Spring Rolls (p.104), Chinese Pork with Water Chestnuts (p.106), Green Pea Soup (p.111), Lamb Samosas (p.122).

Quick and easy
- If you have a few frozen peas left in the packet, try them as a snack!

Tip
- Cold, cooked peas can be added to almost any dish to add colour and flavour.

Can also be used in
Sauce – Tomato (p.72), Butternut Squash Coconut Curry (p.96), Fish Cakes (p.110), Ham Loaf with Pineapple (p.113), Macaroni Cheese (p.124), Spanish Omelette (p.142), Stuffed Peppers with Rice (p.145), Vegetable and Lentil Bake (p.150).

See also
CAULIFLOWER.

PEPPERS (C/U)

RECIPES *Basic:* Crumble/Pie – Vegetable (p.57), Curry (p.58), Pasties – Savoury (p.59), Quiche (p.64), Roasted Vegetables (p.67), Stir-fry (p.74). *Individual:* Baked Potato Fillings (pp.92-3), Chilli Con Carne (p.105), Eggs Over Peppers and Tomatoes (p.109), Lamb Pitta Pockets (p.121), Ratatouille (p.135), Roasted Vegetable Bruschetta (p.136), Stuffed Peppers with Rice (p.145), Roasted Vegetable and Halloumi Kebabs (p.151), Vegetable Stew (p.152).

Quick and easy
- Slice up peppers lengthways and dip in houmous for a quick snack.

Tip
- Green, yellow and red peppers provide great flavour even if they appear a little wrinkly.

Can also be used in
Salad (pp.68-9), Soup (p.73), Vegetable Juices (pp.117-8).

See also
POTATOES, RICE.

PESTO

RECIPES *Basic:* Risotto (p.65).

Quick and easy
- Use it to add flavour to chicken sandwiches
- Use as the basis for a salad dressing (adding lemon juice and a little more oil if needed).
- Mix into freshly cooked pasta and sprinkle with Parmesan for a quick children's tea.

Tip
- Keep in fridge once opened.
- If pesto is too dry, top it up with some olive oil.

See also
LENTILS, NUTS, RUNNER BEANS.

PIE (C)

Tip
- Leftover pie can be reheated, but to avoid it being too dry, serve with a tomato sauce, leftover gravy or green salad with lots of dressing. For sweet pies, serve with custard or cream.

PLUMS (U)

RECIPES *Basic:* Chutney (p.56), Crumble/Pie – Fruit (p.82), Fruit Salad (p.83), Stewed Fruit (p.88).

Quick and easy

- Halve the plums and remove stones. Place in ovenproof dish, sprinkle with sugar and add a little cassis (optional), water and a pinch of ginger. Bake in moderate oven for 20 mins.

Tip

- Local plums, in season, are usually ready to eat, whereas imported plums from the supermarket may be very hard to ripen. To help ripen quickly put unripe fruit in a paper bag with a banana.

PORK (C)

RECIPES *Basic:* Curry (p.58), Meat Pie (p.62), Risotto (p.65), Rissoles (p.66). *Individual:* Chinese Pork with Water Chestnuts (p.106), Pork Enchiladas (p.133).

Quick and easy

- Fry cold pork slices quickly on both sides and served with a green salad and pickle.
- Cold pork makes great sandwiches with either mustard or pickle.

Can also be used in

Sauce – Tomato (p.72), Stock – Meat (p.76).

See also

APPLES.

POTATOES (C/U)

RECIPES *Basic:* Crumble/Pie – Vegetable (p.57), Curry (p.58), Pasties – Savoury (p.59), Chicken/Turkey Pie (p.60), Fish Pie (p.61), Meat Pie (p.62), Shepherd's/Cottage Pie (p.63) (topping), Roasted Vegetables (p.67), Salad (pp.68-9), Soup (p.73). *Individual:* Baked Potato Fillings (pp.92-3), Braised Beef with Winter Vegetables (p.94), Bubble and Squeak (p.95), Butternut Squash Coconut Curry (p.96), Fish Cakes (p.110), Lamb Samosas (p.122), Leek and Potato Soup (p.123), Pottage (p.134), Spanish Omelette (p.142), Sweet Potato and Prawn Cakes (p.146), Vegetable Stew (p.152).

Quick and easy

- Cold roast or baked potatoes can be sliced up and fried in oil with onions – add cooked French beans or red peppers to make a tasty snack.
- Cold mashed potato can be mixed with grated cheese, rolled into croquettes and fried, or used to top a pie.

Tip

- Store potatoes in a dark, cool place.

See also

BAKED POTATO.

POULTRY (C)

RECIPES *Basic:* Chicken/Turkey Pie (p.60), poultry Stock (p.75). *Individual:* see under CHICKEN and TURKEY.

Tip

- Store cold chicken or turkey in an airtight container or freeze it to use later.

Can also be used in

Lamb Pitta Pockets (p.121), Lamb Samosas (p.122).

See also

CHICKEN, TURKEY.

PRAWNS (C)

RECIPES *Basic:* Curry (p.58), Fish Pie (p.61), Risotto (p.65), Stir-fry (p.74). *Individual:* Harissa with Prawns and Couscous (p.115), Sweet Potato and Prawn Cakes (p.146).

Quick and easy
- Prawn and mayonnaise sandwich – the most popular selling sandwich in the UK, and not without reason! Add a squeeze of lemon juice to the mayonnaise.

Tip
- Prawns do not last in the fridge for more than about three days, so plan ahead!

Can also be used in
Salad (pp.68-9), Butternut Squash Coconut Curry (p.96).

See also
BULGUR WHEAT

QUICHE (C)

RECIPES *Basic:* Quiche (p.64).

Quick and easy
- Great for packed lunches.

Tip
- Leftover quiche can be reheated but to avoid it being too dry, serve with a green salad with lots of dressing.

RAISINS (U)

See 'Dried Fruit'.

RASPBERRIES (U)

RECIPES *Basic:* Crumble/Pie – Fruit (p.82), Fruit Salad (p.83), Smoothies (p.86), Fruit Juices (pp.117-9). *Individual:* Mixed Fruit Cheesecake (p.170), Summer Fruits Frozen Yoghurt (p.172), Summer Pudding (p.173).

Quick and easy
- If raspberries are past their best, put them in a juicer and process until smooth. Sieve the juice to remove the pips. Pour over vanilla ice cream.

Tip
- Freeze raspberries on a tray, and transfer frozen berries into a freezer bag.

Can also be used in
Cake Mix (p.80), Blueberry Muffins (p.159).

RHUBARB (C)

RECIPES *Basic:* Crumble/Pie – Fruit (p.82), Pasties – Sweet (p.84), Stewed Fruit (p.88).

Quick and easy
- Leftover cooked rhubarb is delicious on breakfast cereal, or mix with natural yoghurt to make instant rhubarb fool.

Tip
- Add powdered ginger or slices of stemmed ginger to rhubarb when stewing or baking.

Can also be used in
Chutney (p.56), Cake Mix (p.80).

RICE (C)

RECIPES *Basic:* Risotto (p.65), Salad (pp.68-9), Stir-fry (p.74). *Individual:* Chinese Pork with Water Chestnuts (p.106), Kedgeree (p.120), Spicy Sausage Stew (p.144), Stuffed Peppers with Rice (p.145).

Quick and easy
- Add any combination of chopped tomato, red onion, peppers, spring onion, cucumber and sultanas to the cold, cooked rice with a tablespoon of lemon juice and olive oil for a quick rice salad.

Tips
- Freeze cooked rice in self-sealing plastic bags in portions.

- To reheat add 2 tablespoons of water or stock and microwave at full power for 2 minutes, or heat in a saucepan over a high heat – stirring constantly. Make sure the rice is heated right through before serving.
- For safety always cool cooked rice quickly and refrigerate as soon as possible.

See also
BULGUR WHEAT, COUSCOUS, CUCUMBER, DRIED FRUIT, GRAPES, LENTILS, MAYONNAISE, ONIONS, ROASTED VEGETABLES.

RISOTTO (C)

Tip
- Leftover risotto can be reheated but make sure you do it thoroughly.

RISSOLES (C)

Tip
- Leftover rissoles can be crumbled into a pasta sauce or shepherd's/cottage pie.

ROASTED VEGETABLES (C)

RECIPES *Basic:* Soup (p.73). *Individual:* Baked Potato Fillings (pp.92-3), Lamb Pitta Pockets (p.121), Macaroni Cheese (p.124), Roasted Vegetable Bruschetta (p.136).

Quick and easy
- Cold roasted vegetables and houmous, with cracked black pepper make a delicious quick sandwich.
- Add cold roasted vegetables into a rice salad, with some olive oil.

See also
BULGUR WHEAT, COUSCOUS.

RUNNER BEANS (C/U)

RECIPES *Basic:* Chutney (p.56), Curry (p.58), Salad (pp.68-9), Stir-fry (p.74). *Individual:* Butternut Squash Coconut Curry (p.96).

Tip
- Runner beans grow very well in this country so there is often a glut in summer which is a good time to buy them and freeze them for later in the year: 'blanche' the chopped and prepared beans by placing them in boiling water for 2 minutes. Drain fully on kitchen paper and transfer into a freezer bag when cool. Freeze immediately.
- Reheat runner beans in a saucepan in some butter, add a tin of chopped tomatoes and a dollop of pesto or some chopped nuts. For a spicier flavour add a teaspoonful of harissa.

SAUCE (C)

Quick and easy
- Reheat sauce or gravy and pour over meat or vegetables to jazz it up.

Tip
- The addition of a sauce, fresh or reheated, can turn leftover meat, poultry or vegetables into a delicious snack or meal.

Can also be used in
Pies.

SAUSAGES (C)

RECIPES *Basic:* Meat Pie (p.62), Risotto (p.65), Sauce (pp.71-2). *Individual:* Macaroni Cheese (p.124), Spicy Sausage Stew (p.144).

Quick and easy

- Leftover cold sausages are great for a quick snack, either dipped in mustard sauce or between fresh bread for a sausage sandwich. They're also ideal for picnics or packed lunches.

See also
ONIONS.

SMOOTHIE

Tip

- Any leftover smoothie can be poured into a lollie mould to make iced smoothie lollies.

SOUP (C)

Quick and easy

- Leftover soup can be added to a stew, pie or casserole.

SPINACH (C)

RECIPES *Basic:* Quiche (p.64), Soup (p.73), Vegetable Juices (pp.117-8). *Individual:* Pancake Fillings (pp.128-30), Stuffed Peppers with Rice (p.145).

Quick and easy

- Eggs and spinach bake: spread the cooked spinach in an ovenproof dish and cover with cheese sauce and chopped-up hard boiled eggs. Cook until golden brown.

Can also be used in
Stir-fry (p.74).

See also
PANCAKES.

SPRING ONION (U)

RECIPES *Basic:* Salad (pp.68-9), Stir-fry (p.74). *Individual:* Fish Cakes (p.110), Salad Dressing (p.139).

Quick and easy

- Spring onions can be chopped up and added as a garnish to any salad.

Can also be used in
Sweet Potato and Prawn Cakes (p.146).

STIR-FRY (C)

Tip

- Leftover stir-fry can be reheated by microwaving for 60 seconds or heating for 5 minutes in a wok or frying pan, stirring continuously.

STOCK (C)

RECIPES *Basic:* Crumble/Pie – Vegetable (p.57), Chicken/Turkey Pie (p.60), Meat Pie (p.62), Shepherd's/Cottage Pie (p.63), Risotto (p.65), Sauce – Brown (p.71), Soup (p.73), Stock (p.75-8). *Individual:* Braised Beef with Winter Vegetables (p.94), Carrot and Cumin Soup (p.98), Chilli Con Carne (p.105), Green Pea Soup (p.111), Harissa with Prawns and Couscous (p.115), Kedgeree (p.120), Leek and Potato Soup (p.123), Mixed Nut and Tofu Roast (p.126), Pork Enchiladas (p.133), Pottage (p.134), Spicy Sausage Stew (p.144), Vegetable and Lentil Bake (p.150), Vegetable Stew (p.152).

Tips

- Use leftover stock instead of water when cooking rice, couscous or bulgur wheat to add extra flavour.
- Stock freezes well so make your stock when you have a meat, poultry or fish carcass available and freeze to use for another time.

See also
LENTILS.

STRAWBERRIES (U)

RECIPES *Basic:* Fruit Salad (p.83), Smoothies (p.86), Fruit Juices (pp.117-9). *Individual:* Pancake Fillings (pp.128-30), Mixed Fruit Cheesecake (p.170), Summer Fruits Frozen Yoghurt (p.172).

Quick and easy
- Slice up strawberries and serve on top of muesli or breakfast cereal with a dollop of yoghurt.

Tip
- Strawberries don't last very long, even when stored in the fridge so if you have any that may have gone a little soft they could be combined with other soft fruit to make a mixed fruit jam.

Can also be used in
Cake Mix (p.80), Blueberry Muffins (p.159).

SULTANAS
See **DRIED FRUIT**.

SWEDE (C/U)

RECIPES *Basic:* Crumble/Pie – Vegetable (p.57), Curry (p.58), Pasties – Savoury (p.59), Meat Pie (p.62), Rissoles (p.66), Roasted Vegetables (p.67). *Individual:* Braised Beef with Winter Vegetables (p.94), Pottage (p.134), Vegetable Stew (p.152).

Quick and easy
- Fry leftover, mashed swede in butter to make a crispy swede pancake. Serve with lots of black pepper.

Can also be used in
Soup (p.73), Stock – Vegetable (p.78), Butternut Squash Coconut Curry (p.96), Vegetable and Lentil Bake (p.150).

SWEET CORN (TINNED)

RECIPES *Basic:* Crumble/Pie – Vegetable (p.57), Chicken/Turkey Pie (p.60), Salad (pp.68-9). *Individual:* Baked Potato Fillings (pp.92-3), Bubble and Squeak (p.95), Chicken Crunch (p.102), Macaroni Cheese (p.124).

Quick and easy
- Mix up some tinned sweet corn with any leftover chicken or turkey meat and a tablespoon of mayonnaise for a delicious sandwich or baked potato filling.

Can also be used in
Risotto (p.65), Rissoles (p.66), Sauce (pp.70-2).

See also
PASTA.

SWEET POTATO (C/U)

RECIPES *Basic:* Crumble/Pie – Vegetable (p.57), Curry (p.58), Pasties – Savoury (p.59), pies, Roasted Vegetables (p.67), Soup (p.73). *Individual:* Braised Beef with Winter Vegetables (p.94), Sweet Potato and Prawn Cakes (p.146), Vegetable and Lentil Bake (p.150), Vegetable Stew (p.152).

Quick and easy

- Cut sweet potato into wedges, drizzle with oil and chilli powder and bake for 30-45 minutes.

Can also be used in

Baked Potato Fillings (pp.92-3), Butternut Squash Coconut Curry (p.96).

TOMATO (U)

RECIPES *Basic:* Chutney (p.56), Crumble (or Pie) – Vegetable (p.57), Curry (p.58), Quiche (p.64), Roasted Vegetables (p.67), Salad (pp.68-9), Sauce (p.72), Soup (p.73), Vegetable Juices (pp.117-8). *Individual:* Caramelised Onion and Tomato Tart (p.97), Eggs over Peppers and Tomatoes (p.109), Guacamole (p.112), Lamb Pitta Pockets (p.121), Ratatouille (p.135), Roasted Vegetable Bruschetta (p.136), Salad Dressing (p.139), Stuffed Peppers with Rice (p.145), Tomato and Fennel Gazpacho (p.147).

Quick and easy

- Chop up any slightly soft tomatoes in a food processor with half an onion and 1 small chilli (optional) and some lemon juice, to make a delicious salsa. Serve with tortilla chips or as a side serving at barbecues.

Tip

- Keep a few tins of chopped tomatoes in the cupboard for quick pasta sauce.

Can also be used in

Pasties – Savoury (p.59), Fish Cakes (p.110), Macaroni Cheese (p.124).

See also

AVOCADO, BULGUR WHEAT, EGGS, GREENS, KIDNEY BEANS (TINNED), MAYONNAISE, ORANGES, PASTA, RICE, RUNNER BEANS, TUNA.

TUNA (TINNED)

RECIPES *Basic:* Rissoles (p.66), Salad (pp.68-9). *Individual:* Baked Potato Fillings (pp.92-3), Fish Cakes (p.110).

Quick and easy

- Add it to mayonnaise, some chopped-up spring onion and sweet corn to make a delicious sandwich or panini filling.
- Add to cold, cooked pasta with a tin of tomatoes and topped with grated cheese to make quick pasta bake.

Tip

- Once a tin is opened, transfer any unused tuna into a plastic or glass container and cover with clingfilm.

See also

MAYONNAISE, PASTA, YOGHURT.

TURKEY (C)

RECIPES *Basic:* Curry (p.58), Pasties – Savoury (p.59), Chicken/Turkey Pie (p.60), Risotto (p.65), Rissoles (p.66), Salad (pp.68-9), Stir-fry (p.74), Stock (p.75). *Individual:* Chicken Crunch (p.102), Coronation Turkey (p.107), Turkey and Broccoli Hollandaise (p.149).

Quick and easy

- Cold turkey and cranberry sauce sandwiches.

Tip

- If you have a lot of turkey meat leftover after Christmas, freeze it in portions so that it can be used when needed.

Can also be used in

Lamb Pitta Pockets (p.121), Lamb Samosas (p.122).

See also

CHICKEN.

VEGETABLES (C/U)

RECIPES *Basic:* Crumble/Pie – Vegetable (p.57), Pasties – Savoury (p.59), Chicken/Turkey Pie (p.60), Meat Pie (p.62), Shepherd's/Cottage Pie (p.63), Roasted Vegetables (p.67), Soup (p.73), Stir-fry (p.74). *Individual:* Braised Beef with Winter Vegetables (p.94), Spanish Omelette (p.142), Vegetable and Lentil Bake (p.150), Roast Vegetable Kebabs with Halloumi (p.151), Vegetable Stew (p.152).

Tips

- Vegetables still contain a good deal of flavour even when a bit wrinkly and dried out – soups and pies are ideal for using up vegetables left in the rack.
- Vegetables will keep fresh for much longer by wrapping in wet newspaper and storing in a plastic bag in the fridge.

See also

Individual vegetables, e.g. BROAD BEANS, CHICK PEAS.

YOGHURT

RECIPES *Basic:* Curry (p.58), Smoothies (p.86). *Individual:* Banana and Chocolate Digestive Pudding (p.156), Banana and Yoghurt Scotch Pancakes (p.157), Tsatsiki (p.148), Summer Fruits Frozen Yoghurt (p.172).

Quick and easy

- Yoghurt makes a wonderful snack with a spoonful of honey and some chopped banana or nuts.

Tips

- A dollop of natural yoghurt is great on a hot curry, to cool it down, or on any fruit pudding.
- A spoonful of natural yoghurt can be added to mayonnaise to thin it – ideal for making a chicken or tuna sandwich or potato salad.

Can also be used in

Crumble/Pie – Fruit (p.82), Fruit Salad (p.83), Butternut Squash Coconut Curry (p.96), Apple and Cinnamon Fritters (p.154), Blueberry Muffins (p.159), Summer Pudding (p.173).

See also

BISCUITS, CUCUMBER, FRUIT (STEWED), individual fruits e.g. STRAWBERRIES.

Basic Recipes: savoury

that can be adapted for different leftovers

  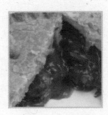 

Ingredients

(alter quantities according to the amount of fruit/vegetables you have).

- 1.5kg of mixed fruit or vegetables
- 3 onions
- 2 cloves of garlic
- Dried fruit (apricots, dates, raisins, sultanas)
- ½ litre of white wine vinegar, cider vinegar or malt vinegar
- 400g of sugar (soft brown or muscovado)
- Some grated ginger
- 1 teaspoon salt
- A spoonful of mixed spice or cinnamon, cloves, Cayenne pepper

Variations

- Apple and pear
- Apple and courgette
- Courgette or marrow and ginger
- Cucumber and apple
- Green tomato and courgette
- Rhubarb and plum

Basic Chutney
Vegetable or fruit

 15 ⏱ 120

Chutney is the most amazing way to use up **fruit** or **vegetables** when you have a glut of them – often at the end of the summer when the courgettes have grown into marrows runner beans, pears and apples are in abundance and everyone is slightly fed up with them. It is also great for using up any tomatoes that you have grown that simply refuse to turn red and remain as little green bullets.

What can go in it?

Although there are some basic ingredients that make up a good chutney, such as white wine or cider vinegar, ginger and onions, the rest of the ingredients can vary according to what you have available and your own particular taste. Having said that, I would always recommend including apples in the ingredients when making a fruit chutney. Avoid damaged or bruised ingredients when making chutney.

Suitable for: Any raw fruit or vegetables e.g. apples, aubergine, apricots, beetroot, blackberries, courgettes, cucumbers, damsons, lemons, mango, marrow, pears, plums, pumpkin, runner beans, rhubarb, tomatoes.

Method

1. Peel, de-seed and chop all the fruit and vegetables and put all the ingredients into a pan and bring to the boil.
2. Then reduce the heat and leave to simmer for about two hours, stirring occasionally, until the fruit and vegetables are really soft and tender. The time taken will depend on the ingredients you are using so test it occasionally. The chutney should have thickened so continue until it has done so.
3. Ladle into sterilised jars, cover the top of the chutney with waxed paper, seal and store in a cool place.
4. Ideally, chutney should be stored for three months or so before being used.

To sterilise jars

Wash jars in hot, soapy water, or put them through the dishwasher cycle. Leave to dry upside down on kitchen paper and then transfer them onto a baking tray and put in a very cool oven (130°C/275°F/gas mark 1) for about 15 minutes. Make sure the jars have close fitting lids or use cellophane with elastic bands.

Lids

Vinegar corrodes metal, so ideally use plastic lids or jars with glass lids.

Basic Crumble/Pie
Vegetable

⏱ 10 ⏱ 75

A vegetable crumble is delicious served in winter or summer either as a meal in itself or as an accompaniment to meat.

What can go in it?

Any combination of **vegetables** will do but I have suggested groupings that tie in with the seasons, making this an economical, as well as a very tasty, dish. Instead of a crumble topping, try pastry for a vegetable pie.

Suitable for: (For winter vegetable crumble): broccoli, cabbage, carrots, leeks, parsnips, swede, sweet potato, turnips. (For summer vegetable crumble): aubergine, courgettes, red peppers, tomatoes.

Method

1 Preheat oven to 180°C/350°F/gas mark 4.

2 Make your shortcrust pastry (p.89), put it in a plastic bag in the fridge for an hour.

3 Dice or chop the vegetables. Slice the onion and melt the butter in a casserole dish, fry the chopped onion for about 3 minutes until soft. Stir in the flour, removing as many lumps as possible gradually adding in the stock stirring all the time until you have a smooth sauce.

4 Add the chopped vegetables, tomato purée, horseradish sauce and salt and pepper, cover with a lid and place in the oven for 45 minutes.

5 For the topping, put the flour or combination of flour and oats in a bowl and chop up the butter into the flour.

6 Using your hands, gradually blend the butter into the flour until it is evenly distributed and the mixture looks like breadcrumbs.

7 Scatter topping over vegetables and bake for 30 minutes.

Instead of a crumble topping, you can use shortcrust pastry to make a pie topping. Roll out the pastry, lay over the dish and cook for 35 minutes at 200°C/400°F/gas mark 6.

Ingredients

- 400g of a combination of the above vegetables
- 2 onions
- 25g margarine or butter
- 1 tablespoon flour
- 300ml vegetable stock
- 30ml horseradish sauce (optional)

For crumble topping

- 200g plain flour or 200g of a combination of flour and oats, flour and muesli, flour and crumbled biscuits
- 75g butter, room temperature

For pastry topping

- 200g shortcrust pastry (or 200g pre-made pastry)

Variations

Topping
pastry topping

Basic Curry

 10 ⏱ 70

'Curry' is a word that covers a wide range of dishes and there are numerous varieties but this is a basic curry recipe which provides the platform to which other flavours can be added.

What can go in it?

Curries are fast becoming a great 'British' dish and they are so adaptable that just about any meat or vegetable can be added, raw or cooked. If you have time, prepare your curry well in advance and reheat before eating – this improves the flavour – although meat curries should only be reheated once.

This recipe can form the basis of your curry dish from which to experiment with different ingredients. For a tangy flavour, you might try adding some **natural yoghurt** to the sauce, or you can make a more tomato-based curry by adding a tin of **chopped tomatoes**.

Suitable for: Bite-sized pieces of cooked or raw beef, chicken, pork or turkey; cooked or raw prawns; cooked or raw vegetables: butternut squash, broad beans, carrots, cauliflower, courgettes, leeks, mushrooms, peas, peppers, swede, tomatoes; cooked potatoes.

Method

1. In a wok or frying pan, heat the oil over a high heat. Add the onion and fry for a couple of minutes. Then add the garlic.
2. Add any raw meat and cook for a further 5 minutes. (Skip this if you are using cooked meat.)
3. Add any raw vegetables and cook for 5 minutes, stirring all the time
4. Add the curry powder or spices. Stir well.
5. Add any cooked meat and vegetables and stir well to ensure they are coated in the curry powder or spices.
6. Add tomato purée and stir in well to ensure all the spices are absorbed.
7. Cover and simmer on a low heat for one hour.
8. Just before serving, add the double cream or crème fraîche and mix in well.
9. Garnish with fresh coriander leaves.

Ingredients

- 500g of any of the leftovers (see right).
- Olive or sesame oil for cooking
- Chopped onion
- About 2 cloves garlic, crushed
- Tomato purée
- A pinch of salt
- Curry powder (about 2 teaspoons or to taste) or ½ teaspoon cumin; ¼ teaspoon turmeric; ¼ teaspoon coriander; ¼ teaspoon garam masala
- ½ green chilli, chopped and de-seeded (or adjust according to taste)
- Double cream or crème fraîche

Basic Pasty
Savoury

⏱ 10 ⏱ 60

Tradition claims that the pasty was originally made as lunch for Cornish tin miners who could hold the pasty by the folded crust and eat the rest, discarding the dirty pastry. In such pasties, the meat and each vegetable would have its own pastry compartment and some pasties would have the meat and vegetables at one end and the fruit 'pudding' at the other.

Pasties are a great way to use up savoury or sweet leftovers and the beauty of the pasty is that the filling does not have to be cooked before making.

What can go in it?

Just about any finely chopped or minced raw meat, vegetables or cheeses can be used in the filling. With savoury pasties adding herbs is important for enhancing the flavour.

Suitable for: a mixture of any of the following vegetables: carrots, leeks, peas, swede, turnip, sweet potato, tomatoes.

Method

❶ Preheat the oven to 180°C/350°F/gas mark 4.
❷ Make your shortcrust pastry (p.89), put it in a plastic bag in the fridge for an hour.
❸ Divide pastry into 4 equal pieces and roll each piece out until it is about ½cm thick and you can cut out a circle from it about 20cm in diameter (using a plate).
❹ In a bowl, mix all the filling ingredients and then divide the filling into 4 and spoon it out across the middle of the pastry circles. Season well.
❺ Brush the edges of the circles with milk and then bring up the edges to the centre covering the filling. Carefully, using your thumb and forefingers, crimp the edge to form a sealed crest along the top of the pasty, making sure you have left no holes.
❻ When you have done all 4 pasties, lay them on a baking sheet and chill for 30 minutes.
❼ Glaze with milk or beaten egg, then bake in the oven for 1 hour.

Ingredients: (for 4 pasties)

For the filling: (savoury)
- 500g shortcrust pastry
- 500-600g of any combination of: raw meat (finely chopped or minced), vegetables, pulses, beans or cheese.
- 1 onion, finely chopped
- Fresh parsley, rosemary, thyme or basil (depending on what your ingredients are)
- Turmeric and ginger for a spicy pasty
- Black pepper

Variations

Fillings
- Goat's cheese
- Red pepper and basil
- Lamb, mint and onion
- Cheese and onion
- Lentil and vegetable

Pastry
- Puff pastry

Basic Pie
Chicken/turkey

⏱ 15 ⏱ 20/40

The beauty of this pie is that virtually all the remains of the traditional British main course can go into it! It is particularly good after Christmas when so much good food is often thrown away, or after a Sunday roast.

What can go in it?

This is a classic scraps recipe after roast **chicken** or **turkey** using up all the leftover vegetables, gravy, any meat picked off the carcass and the carcass itself to make a stock for the sauce. It may not be realistic to use all the optional ingredients listed below although leeks do add a particularly good taste. Some good combinations of vegetables for a poultry pie are **leeks** and **carrots** (adding cheese to the white sauce); leeks and **mushrooms**; carrots and **sweet corn** or **peas** and carrots.

Suitable for: Chicken, turkey; broccoli, carrots, leeks, peas; gravy; wine.

Method

1. Preheat the oven to 200°C/400°F/gas mark 6.
2. Make your shortcrust pastry (p.89). Put it in a plastic bag in the fridge for an hour.
3. Fry up the bacon pieces (packs of cheap bacon pieces are perfect for this). Then fry the onion in the bacon fat, until it softens. Add any raw vegetables and cook for 2 minutes.
4. To make the sauce, melt the butter in a saucepan and add the flour and mix in to remove as many lumps as possible.
5. Gradually blend in the stock/milk (and wine if you are using it), stirring constantly over a medium heat until the sauce becomes thick and smooth.
6. Stir in any leftover cooked vegetables and cooked chicken or turkey, season with salt and pepper, perhaps add some herbs such as tarragon, and transfer to an ovenproof pie dish.
7. For a pastry topping, roll out shortcrust pastry a little larger than the dish, cover the dish with the pastry and press down around the lip of the dish. Dampen the edges so they stick down well. Pierce a hole in the top to allow steam to escape. Glaze with milk or beaten egg.
8. Alternatively, add a topping of mashed potato or raw, sliced potatoes.
9. For pastry or raw potatoes, cook pie in the oven for 30 minutes or until the pastry is cooked. If using mashed or cooked potato, cook for 25 minutes until potato has turned golden.

Ingredients

- 500g chicken or turkey meat
- Bacon or ham, if you have any (cooked or raw)
- 450g shortcrust pastry
- 1 onion, chopped
- Any amount of leeks, broccoli, carrots, peas (cooked or raw), tin of sweet corn (optional)
- Mushrooms, chopped (optional)
- Tarragon (optional)

For the sauce

- 2 tablespoons flour
- 50g butter
- 500ml stock (750ml if not using milk)
- 250ml milk (optional),
- 100ml white wine (optional)
- Salt & pepper

Variations

Topping
- Puff pastry
- Mashed potato
- Sliced potato

Basic Pie
Fish

 15-20  20-35

With leftover fish only lasting in the fridge for a matter of 2-3 days, fish pie is an easy way to scoop up all the leftovers at once. Fish pie is also great to freeze, as long as any cooked fish you use has not been frozen before – it is fine if the fish was frozen when raw.

What can go in it?

Virtually any kind of fish or **shellfish** can be added to a fish pie and the more variety the better – **squid**, **mussels** and **prawns** and **smoked fish** make the pie extra tasty and it's also possible to add cooked or frozen peas or cooked, diced carrots.

Suitable for: Cooked or raw fish or shellfish; smoked fish; cooked mashed or boiled potato; cooked carrots or peas.

Method

❶ Preheat the oven to 200°C/400°F/gas mark 6.

❷ Make your shortcrust pastry (p.89). Put it in a plastic bag in the fridge for an hour.

❸ If using raw fish, poach the fish in the milk and bay leaf for about 5 minutes. Keep the milk to make the sauce.

❹ Transfer cooked fish to a pie dish and flake it using the back of a fork (or cut up prawns or squid etc. to bite size bits), removing any stray bones. Add any cooked carrots or peas to the fish and sliced up hard boiled eggs.

❺ To make the sauce, melt the butter in a saucepan, add the flour and mix well to make a paste. Gradually blend in the milk (from the poaching or fresh milk if using cooked fish), stirring all the time until you have a smooth sauce. Add salt, pepper and dill.

❻ Pour sauce over the fish and mix in well.

❼ For a potato topping, either use cooked mashed potato over the top with 3 or 4 little knobs of butter on top, or sliced up boiled potatoes.

❽ For a pastry topping, roll out the shortcrust or puff pastry a little larger than the dish, cover the dish with the pastry and press down around the lip of the dish. Dampen the edges so they stick down well. Pierce a hole in the top to allow the steam to escape and glaze with milk or beaten egg.

Cooking times

Potato topping: cooked potatoes: 20 minutes
  uncooked potatoes: 35 minutes
Pastry topping: 30 – 35 minutes

Ingredients

- 700g cooked or raw fish or shellfish (eg smoked haddock, cod, prawns, squid etc.)
- 450g shortcrust pastry
- 3 hard boiled eggs
- Milk and one bay leaf (if poaching raw fish)
- Cooked peas and carrots, diced (optional)
- Salt and pepper

For the white sauce

- 50g butter
- 2 tablespoons flour
- 300ml milk
- 1 teaspoon dill

For the topping

- 500g mashed potato or equivalent sliced up boiled potatoes
- Grated cheese (optional)

Variations

Topping
- Puff pastry
- Sliced potatoes

Basic Pie
Meat

🕐 15 🕐 20/40

A meat pie makes an ideal home for leftover cooked meat and makes a delicious Sunday lunch recipe on cold, winter weekends. Alternatively, make little individual pies for children's teas or suppers for one in front of the telly.

What can go in it?

Just about any cooked meat or combination of meats can be used, including **sausages**, **offal** and **game**, as well as **lamb**, **beef** and **pork**. Diced, minced or cut into strips, the meat can be combined with any number of cooked or raw vegetables and the addition of pulses, such as **lentils** or **cooked flageolet** or **cannelloni beans**, provides substance as well as flavour. If you have any leftover **ale** or **stout** or the last dregs of a Marmite, Bovril or Vegemite pot then add that to the sauce as well.

Suitable for: Cooked beef, lamb or pork; cooked or raw vegetables: carrots, leeks, mushrooms, peas, swede; cooked pulses; leftover ale or stout, Marmite, Bovril or Vegemite.

Method

❶ Preheat the oven to 200°C/400°F/gas mark 6.

❷ Make your shortcrust pastry (p.89). Put it in a plastic bag in the fridge for an hour.

❸ Melt the butter in a casserole dish. Fry the chopped onion and garlic for about 3 minutes until soft.

❹ Add the raw vegetables and cook for a further 2 minutes, stirring constantly.

❺ Stir in the flour, then gradually add the stock and red wine or beer, if using, stirring all the time until the sauce thickens.

❻ Add the cooked meat, tinned tomatoes (if using) and any cooked vegetables. Mix well and add salt and pepper to taste.

❼ For a pastry topping: roll out the pastry a little larger than the dish, cover the dish with the pastry and press down around the lip of the dish. Dampen the edges so they stick down well. Pierce a hole in the top to allow steam to escape. Glaze with milk or beaten egg.

❽ Alternatively, slice up cooked or raw potatoes and cover the top of the pie, brushing the potatoes with milk will create a nice glaze on cooking. Equally, use up any leftover mashed potato as a topping instead.

❾ For a pastry or raw potato topping, bake the pie in the oven for 30 minutes. For a mashed or cooked potato topping, bake for 20 minutes or until topping starts to brown.

Ingredients

- 500g of cooked meat (or combination of meat and pulses)
- 450g shortcrust pastry
- Raw or cooked vegetables, chopped
- Tin of flageolet or cannelloni beans (optional)
- Tinned tomatoes (optional)
- Worcestershire sauce
- Salt and pepper to taste

For the sauce

- 1 tablespoon butter
- 2 onions
- 1 or 2 cloves garlic
- 1 tablespoon flour
- 1 pint brown (meat) stock
- ½ glass of red wine/1 glass of ale or stout (if available)

Variations

Topping

- Puff pastry
- Mashed potato
- Sliced potato

Basic Pie
Shepherd's pie/Cottage pie

🕐 20 🕐 45

Traditionally, cottage pie is made up with beef, whilst shepherd's pie is made with lamb. These pies are a great way of 'losing' vegetables – especially if you have fussy eaters in the house who are a bit reticent with their '5 a day'.

What can go in it?

There are lots of things you can add to bulk up the pie or give it flavour – **baked beans** are a favourite in our family but pulses such as **flageolet** or **cannelloni beans** are also tasty. Leftover cooked **carrots, runner or broad beans** and **peas** are particularly good and try adding some **mushrooms** as well. If you have an empty Marmite, Bovril or Vegemite pot, add boiling water, give the pot a good shake and this makes lovely stock for your pie. Alternatively, add any leftover gravy from a roast.

Suitable for: Cooked, minced (or finely chopped) beef or lamb; cooked or raw vegetables: carrots, peas, runner or broad beans; tinned baked beans; leftover mashed potato; leftover gravy; cooked pulses.

Method

1. Preheat the oven to 180°C/350°F/gas mark 4.
2. Fry the onion in the dripping or oil until it's just turning golden but not burnt.
3. Add the mince and carrots and any other raw vegetables and stir until the mixture is heated through – don't worry that the vegetables aren't soft yet. Add the stock/gravy and let it simmer for 15 minutes.
4. Add any cooked vegetables/pulses and mix well. Pour into an ovenproof or Pyrex dish.
5. Spread the mashed potato or chopped up leftover roast or boiled potatoes evenly over the meat in the dish.
6. Bake in the oven for at least 40 minutes until the potato is golden and serve immediately.

Ingredients

- 500g leftover roasted joint of lamb or beef, minced (or finely chopped)
- 500g raw potatoes for mashing (or leftover mashed potato or chopped-up leftover roast or sliced potatoes)
- Knob of dripping or some vegetable oil for cooking
- 1 large onion, finely chopped
- Carrots (leftover or raw), chopped and any other leftover raw or cooked vegetables
- ½ pint of stock and/or gravy
- A tin of pulses or baked beans (optional)

Variations

Toppings
- Sliced potatoes
- Leftover sliced roast potatoes
- Mashed potatoes

Ingredients

- Any combination of the leftover ingredients (see right)
- A good chunk of grated cheese (preferably Gruyère but Cheddar will do)
- 2 eggs
- 2 egg yolks
- 250ml milk
- 125ml double cream
- Salt and pepper to taste
- Pinch grated nutmeg
- 400g shortcrust pastry

Variations

- Bacon
- Ham and mushroom
- Courgette and red pepper
- Mixed vegetable
- Ricotta and spinach
- Smoked salmon and broccoli

Basic Quiche

⏲ 10 +15 ⏲ 30

A quiche is delicious hot or cold, served up as part of a picnic or eaten with a green salad and new potatoes in the summer. It will even freeze well, making it an all-round versatile dish.

What can go in it?

Quiches are perfect for using up virtually any combination of leftover meat and vegetables, and can be eaten cold or hot. Quiches can be frozen, so if you have a glut of vegetables it is a good way of using them up and eating them at a later date.

Suitable for: Cooked, chopped bacon or ham; smoked fish; cooked vegetables: broccoli, courgettes, leeks, mushrooms, onion, peas, peppers, spinach, tomatoes; cheese.

You will need a 25cm flan dish.

Method

❶ Preheat the oven to 190°C/375°F/gas mark 5.

❷ Make your shortcrust pastry (p.89). Put it in a plastic bag in the fridge for an hour.

❸ Roll out the pastry a little larger than the greased flan dish. Line the dish with the pastry, pushing it down so it sticks to the rim and sides. Cut the excess pastry off.

❹ Use a fork to make some holes in the base and cook for 15 minutes. Alternatively, use a pre-cooked pastry case placed on an oven tray.

❺ Line the base of the flan case with any of your extra ingredients (see above) so that they are evenly spread out.

❻ Put the eggs, egg yolks, milk, cream, salt and pepper and nutmeg in a bowl and whisk together well.

❼ Pour over the added ingredients inside the flan case.

❽ Bake in the oven for about 25-30 minutes until the quiche mixture has set and slightly browned on the top.

Basic Risotto

⏱ 10 ⏱ 30

Whilst risotto is best eaten immediately after cooking, it is possible to freeze it, although take care that you reheat the rice quickly and thoroughly and, if you are using any cooked meat, be sure that the meat has not previously been frozen in its cooked state.

What can go in it?

While you can use all kinds of cooked or raw leftovers in risotto, it is best to use **uncooked rice** as the flavours are absorbed by the rice during the cooking process. Risottos are most successful using **Italian Arborio rice**. Try adding a dollop of **pesto** on top of each helping of risotto – it's delicious.

Suitable for: Cooked bacon, beef, ham, lamb, pork, poultry or prawns; cooked or raw vegetables: beans, broccoli, carrots, leeks, mushrooms, peas, sweet corn.

Method

❶ Heat up the stock (vegetable or chicken) in a saucepan. Allow it to simmer with the lid on to keep it from evaporating.

❷ Heat the olive oil in a large saucepan, add the onions and fry gently until soft but not coloured. Add the garlic and continue to cook for 1 minute or so.

❸ Add the rice and stir until coated with oil. Let it cook for 1 minute, being careful not to let it burn.

❹ Add the wine, if using, then turn heat right down and let it simmer until the wine has been absorbed.

❺ Now add a couple of ladles of stock. Stir and let it simmer again until the stock has been absorbed.

❻ Repeat this until you have finished the stock. The rice should be cooked by now, firm and glossy but not sticky.

❼ Add a handful of Parmesan and stir it round and serve, adding a squeeze of lemon and some cracked, black pepper and a bit more Parmesan, and perhaps a spoonful of pesto, to each serving.

Ingredients

- 300g of any of the suitable leftovers (see left)
- 2 tablespoons olive oil
- 1 or 2 onions, finely chopped
- 1 or 2 garlic cloves, crushed
- 1 handful of Arborio or other short-grain Italian rice per person
- Glass of white wine (optional)
- 1 litre stock
- Parmesan, grated
- A squeeze of lemon

Ingredients

- 500g cooked meat or poultry or unsalted, finely chopped mixed nuts
- 1 onion, finely chopped
- 3 tablespoons breadcrumbs
- Salt and pepper to taste
- Fresh or dried parsley
- Fresh or dried rosemary
- 1 clove garlic, crushed
- 1 teaspoon Tabasco sauce (optional)
- 1 teaspoon tomato purée
- 1 egg, beaten
- Flour, seasoned with salt and pepper
- Vegetable or olive oil for cooking

Variations

- Beef and onion
- Chicken and sweet corn
- Lamb and rosemary
- Mixed nuts
- Tuna

Basic Rissoles

 15 10-15

Rissoles can be frozen so long as any meat you use in them has not been frozen in its cooked form. Be careful how you store rissoles in the freezer, though, as they are delicate and can be easily crushed. The best way is to store them between layers of greaseproof paper, in a deep, plastic container.

What can go in it?

Rissoles are an old fashioned dish invented for using up **leftover meat** or **poultry** in a way that was quick, easy and not expensive, using only store cupboard ingredients. The vegetarian option of using **nuts** is also delicious.

Suitable for: Leftover cooked meat or poultry; cooked or raw vegetables: carrots, leeks, peas, sweet corn, swede; nuts; stale bread (breadcrumbs).

Method

❶ Mix all the ingredients (except the flour and oil) in a large bowl.
❷ Divide up the mixture into 8 and roll into balls.
❸ With floured hands, roll each ball in the seasoned flour, working on the ball to remove any cracks that might cause the rissole to fall apart when it is cooking.
❹ Heat the oil in a frying pan over a medium heat. When the oil is hot, add the rissoles and fry for about 10 minutes, turning occasionally, until golden-brown all over and cooked.
❺ Serve immediately on a bed of salad or with seasonal vegetables.

Basic Roasted Vegetables

⏱ 10 ⏱ 25

This is one of the most delicious ways to serve vegetables as it combines different textures and tastes and none of the goodness or taste is lost in cooking. A really good olive oil enhances the flavour and fragrance, as does the use of fresh, rather than dried herbs, particularly fresh rosemary and thyme. If there are any leftovers keep them in the fridge – they can either be eaten cold, or put inside warm pitta bread, on a baked potato or added to a salad.

What can go in it?

The beauty of this dish is that you don't need more than one of each type of vegetable so it is the perfect recipe for a quick sweep around the vegetable rack – clearing the decks before you go shopping again. Try to vary the colours and textures of the vegetables: one good combination is **courgettes** with **peppers** and **baby corn** which provide a crunchy texture as well as a bright yellow colour.

Suitable for: Most raw vegetables including aubergines, carrots, cherry tomatoes, courgettes, leeks, mini sweet corn, parsnips, potatoes, red onions (or shallots), red or yellow peppers, sweet potato, swede, turnip.

Method

❶ Preheat the oven to 220°C/425°F/gas mark 7.
❷ Roughly chop (and de-seed where necessary) all the vegetables and spread them out on a baking tray.
❸ Pour a really big slug of olive oil over the vegetables. Then, using your (clean) hands, mix the vegetables so that they are all well coated in oil.
❹ Arrange the thyme and rosemary over the vegetables and add black pepper as required.
❺ Cook in the oven for about 25 minutes or until all the vegetables are browning and turning crispy on top. It is a good idea to take the tray out of the oven occasionally and mix the vegetables up with a spoon to ensure even cooking.
❻ Serve immediately hot – or they are just as delicious cold.

Ingredients

- Any combination of the vegetables (see left)
- Good quality olive oil
- About 2 cloves garlic, quartered
- 2 sprigs rosemary
- 4 sprigs thyme
- Black pepper

Basic Salad

There are an infinite number of varieties and combinations of salad, and you can use meat, poultry, fish, vegetables and even fruit, but nothing beats a simple bowl of fresh green leaves with a good dressing; whilst the ingredients of the salad are important, the quality of the dressing can make all the difference to the taste. Here are just a few suggestions for salads and dressings to serve with them:

Waldorf salad

 10

Suitable for: Apple and celery.
❶ Dice up some apple and celery and add walnuts and raisins.
❷ Mix with a dressing and serve immediately or store in a sealed container, having sprinkled the apple with lemon juice to stop it from going brown.

Dressing suggestion: Mayonnaise with lemon juice and black pepper.

Easy potato salad

 5

Suitable for: Cooked boiled potatoes.
❶ Cut the potatoes into bite-size chunks.
❷ Mix with a dressing and some chopped chives.

Dressing suggestion: Mayonnaise with a crushed clove of garlic, lemon juice, Dijon mustard and tarragon.

Rice salad

⏱ 10

Suitable for: Cold, cooked rice, couscous.
❶ Mix the cold rice with chopped tomatoes, red peppers, cucumber, raisins and halved walnuts, and mix with dressing.
❷ To spice it up, try adding a teaspoon of harissa sauce or some cold, cooked green beans and a little chilli oil.
❸ Garnish with black olives.
❹ This also works well with bulgur wheat or couscous.

Dressing suggestion: Lemon vinaigrette.

Pasta salad

 10

Suitable for: Cooked pasta (almost any shape will do except for lasagne, spaghetti or tagliatelle).

❶ Combine the cold, cooked pasta with any of the following: halved cherry tomatoes, chopped up cooked bacon, cubed cucumber, finely chopped raw red onion, shredded raw red cabbage, chopped raw red pepper, dried fruit, nuts.

❷ You could also add a spoonful of pesto and mix it in well with the pasta.

Dressing suggestion: lemon vinaigrette, mayonnaise with lemon juice and black pepper or, for a bit more kick, add a little chilli oil.

Three bean salad

 5

Suitable for: Tinned pulses; cold, cooked green or runner beans.

❶ Use any combination of tinned kidney, cannelloni, flageolet or black eyed beans and a chopped raw red pepper and finely chopped raw red onion, plus a good squeeze of fresh lemon juice.

❷ Any cold, cooked green or runner beans can be added as well.

Dressing suggestion: Lemon vinaigrette.

Green bean salad

10

Suitable for: Green beans or cold, cooked beans.

❶ Either steam your French beans for a few minutes until cooked but still crunchy, or use leftover cooked beans. Make sure they are dry by patting them with kitchen paper.

Dressing suggestion: Olive oil and mint dressing: Heat a tablespoon of olive oil in a frying pan and fry 3 cloves of garlic (sliced) until crisp and golden. Allow to cool, then add 2 more tablespoons of oil, 1 tablespoon of balsamic vinegar and 3 tablespoons of chopped up mint.

Ingredients

- 50g butter
- 2 tablespoons flour
- 250ml milk
- Salt and pepper
- ½ teaspoon grainy mustard (optional)

Variations

Cheese sauce
- Add 50g Cheddar cheese

Parsley sauce
- Add 2 tablespoons finely chopped parsley

Mushroom sauce
- Cook 100g thinly sliced mushrooms in melted butter until soft and add to the sauce, using, if possible the mushroom butter to make the sauce

Egg and mustard sauce
- Finely chop three hardboiled eggs and add them to the sauce, along with 1 teaspoon of English mustard

Rich white sauce
- Whisk 1 egg yolk with 2 tablespoons of cream and then mix into the white sauce.

Basic Sauce
White

 2 5

A white sauce is the basis for so many pies and dishes and can also transform cooked leftovers into a delicious meal. It is therefore an extremely important part of the leftover pioneer's repertoire! Variations of white sauce can be used with all kinds of cooked vegetables, such as **broccoli**, **cauliflower** and **leeks**, with cooked **poultry** or **ham** and **pasta** e.g. **macaroni** or **lasagne**.

The ingredients for a white sauce all come from the store cupboard – it's a good idea to keep it stocked up.

Use with: Cooked poultry, ham or bacon; cooked vegetables: broccoli, cauliflower, leeks, mushrooms, peppers; cheese, cooked macaroni.

Method

1. Melt the butter in a saucepan.
2. Add the flour and mix well until the butter and flour form a ball and leave the sides of the pan – do not allow to go brown.
3. Gradually blend in the milk, stirring constantly over a medium heat until the sauce becomes thick and smooth.
4. Bring to the boil and cook for 1-2 minutes. Season with salt and pepper.

Basic Sauce
Brown (gravy)

⏱ 5 ⏱ 10

Brown sauce is basically a thickened meat based stock which can either be used in a **meat pie**, **stew** or **casserole** or poured over vegetables for a **vegetable pie**. Leftover, cooked meat can sometimes become rather dried out, so pouring a brown sauce over it can resurrect it.

Use with: Cooked meat; winter vegetables e.g. carrot, butternut squash, swede, sweet potato, turnip.

Method

❶ Melt the butter in a saucepan. Fry the chopped onion for about 3 minutes until soft.
❷ Add the garlic and mushrooms and fry for a further 2 minutes.
❸ Stir in the flour, removing as many lumps as possible.
❹ Add the stock and red wine or beer and bring the mixture to the boil.
❺ Reduce the heat, add salt and pepper and let the sauce simmer for about 10-15 minutes until the sauce has reduced by about half.
❻ The sauce is then ready to be used for pies and stews.

Ingredients

- 50g butter
- 1 onion, chopped
- Handful of mushrooms (optional)
- 1 clove garlic
- 1 tablespoon flour
- 1 pint meat (brown) stock
- ½ glass red wine/1 glass ale or stout (optional)
- Salt and pepper

Basic Sauce
Tomato

 5 20

A basic tomato sauce can be added to any pasta or rice dish or on a baked potato, and a variety of other leftover ingredients can be added, which makes it an ideal dish for using up leftovers. Tomato sauce can be frozen, so if you have lots of leftovers around, make the sauce and freeze it in portions to use when you need it. Tomato sauce is greatly enhanced by adding **fresh basil leaves**. These are fragile and turn brown quickly, so keep them on short stems, rinse and dry gently on paper towels, and store them in a large plastic bag with air trapped inside, then refrigerate.

What can go in it?

A variety of raw or cooked vegetables, or cooked meat, is delicious in a tomato sauce. Chorizo or pepperoni will give extra bite to your sauce.

Suitable for: slightly overripe tomatoes, leftover cooked meat, ham, bacon or chicken, leftover salami or chorizo, raw or cooked vegetables.

Method

1. Heat the oil in a saucepan or frying pan and add the onion and garlic.
2. Cook for about 3 minutes until the onion and garlic are soft.
3. Add any raw vegetables, chopped and cook for 4 minutes stirring continually.
4. Add the tinned tomatoes and stir in.
5. Add any of the cooked meat or vegetables and heat through for about 10 minutes. Season with black pepper.
6. Add the chopped basil leaves, or dried basil.

Ingredients

- 1 tablespoon of olive oil
- 1 onion, chopped
- 1 clove garlic, chopped
- 400g tin of chopped tomatoes or 4 large tomatoes, chopped
- Black pepper
- 8 basil leaves or 2 teaspoons dried basil
- Grated Parmesan to taste

Plus any of the following

Cooked
- Chicken
- Turkey
- Pork or beef chopped or minced
- Sausage
- Salami
- Ham or chorizo, sliced

Cooked or raw:
- Broccoli
- Carrots
- Courgettes
- Leeks
- Mushrooms
- Peas
- Runner beans
- Sweet corn

Basic Soup

⏱ 10 ⏱ 20

Soups are quick and easy to make and provide an instant meal or snack served with a thick slice of fresh bread – ideal for when you have unexpected visitors. Depending on the ingredients, the soup can either be blended smooth or, especially for meat-based soups, left chunky for a really hearty meal.

What can go in it?

Soup is ideal for both leftover cooked and raw vegetables and cooked meat or poultry, and even cheese, and you can make a more hearty soup by adding pulses, e.g. lentils, butter beans or chick peas, and add flavour with herbs and spices.

The secret is a good stock, ideally home-made (see Basic Stock recipe), or made using good quality stock cubes. It is best, but not essential, to use chicken stock for chicken soup, meat stock for a meat-based soup and so on. Chicken stock for a vegetable soup is fine as long as you supplement the soup with plenty of strong tasting vegetables and are not serving vegetarians.

The variations are endless and some combinations work better than others, so experiment!

Suitable for: Cooked poultry or meat; cooked or raw vegetables: beans, broccoli, butterbeans, butternut squash, cabbage, carrots, courgettes, leeks, mushrooms, onions, parsnips, peas, peppers, potatoes, pulses, spinach, swede, sweet potato, turnip; cheese.

Method

① Melt the butter in a saucepan and add the garlic, onion, potato if using, and any raw vegetables you want to use. Cook for 5 minutes, stirring constantly.
② Add herbs or curry powder or other spices if using and cook for a further 3 minutes, mixing it in well.
③ Add the stock, leftover meat/poultry/cooked vegetables/cheeses, and salt and pepper.
④ Simmer for 15-20 minutes, depending on which vegetables you're using.
⑤ Liquidise if you like a smooth soup.
⑥ Garnish with parsley or coriander and add cream if you wish.

Ingredients

- 25g butter
- 1 or 2 onions, diced
- 1 clove garlic, finely chopped
- 1 or 2 potatoes, diced (if you want a thicker soup)
- 1 litre of stock or water
- Herbs to taste
- 1 teaspoon curry powder (optional)
- Salt and pepper to taste
- Cream (optional)
- 600-700g of whichever leftovers you want to use up

Variations

- Carrot and coriander
- Carrot and orange
- Onion and potato
  Broccoli and stilton
- Chicken and leek
- Sausage and bean
- Bacon, carrot and butterbean
  Beef and cabbage
- Add 1 teaspoon curry powder to add spicy flavour.

Basic Stir-fry

⏱ 10 ⏱ 15-20

Not only are stir-fries quick and easy but they are extremely healthy as the food is cooked at very high temperatures so that very little goodness is lost from the vegetables.

What can go in it?

This is ideal for almost any raw vegetables as well as raw or cooked **meat**, **poultry** or **prawns** and cold, cooked **rice**. Although cooked vegetables such as **carrots**, **mange tout** or **peppers** can be used, for best results use **raw vegetables** as the point of a stir-fry is that the vegetables are cooked at a very high temperature so that they remain crisp. Chinese vegetables such as **pak choi** and **Chinese flowering cabbage (choi sum)** are made for this type of recipe so try experimenting by adding these along side your leftovers.

For extra flavour, try using sesame oil instead of normal vegetable or olive oil as it gives off a lovely aroma and provides a nutty taste. You could also try marinating any raw meat, poultry or prawns in soy sauce for a few hours before cooking.

Suitable for: Cooked or raw beef, pork, chicken, prawns; raw or cooked vegetables: baby corn, bean sprouts, broccoli, carrots, cauliflower, celery, choi sum, courgette, French beans, leeks, mange tout, mushrooms, pak choi, red peppers, spring onions, yellow peppers; cooked rice.

Method

❶ Heat the oil over a high heat in a wok or frying pan.
❷ Add any uncooked meat, poultry or prawns and fry for about 3 minutes, stirring constantly.
❸ Add other vegetables, chillies, spring onions and ginger, and fry for a further 10 minutes, tossing the vegetables all the time.
❹ Add any cooked meat, poultry or prawns and any cold, cooked rice and carry on stir-frying until these are warmed through (about 3-4 minutes).
❺ Add the soy sauce and stir so that it is well mixed in.
❻ Serve immediately with a dash of fresh lemon or lime.

Ingredients

- 400g of any mixture of the ingredients (see right), chopped or sliced
- 2 tablespoons sesame oil (or vegetable oil)
- Fresh ginger, grated
- Spring onions
- Red chillies, finely chopped (optional)
- Any leftover cold rice (optional)
- 2 tablespoons dark soy sauce
- Squeeze of lemon/lime

Variations

- Chicken and cashew nuts
- Beef and chilli
- Chicken with oyster sauce
- Prawn and sweet chilli sauce

Basic Stock
Poultry

⏱ 10 ⏱ 120-180

A good, strong stock, made from raw or cooked meat or poultry carcasses provides the ideal backbone to making just about any soup you like. Stock is also very useful when making a sauce or in stews, adding extra flavour and substance. All the excess flesh should be stripped from the carcass and then the bones can be used for the stock, so don't throw it away. It is essential for all stocks that a large saucepan is used and that the bones are always well covered with water. Always leave the stock to cool and scrape the hard fat off the top before using. This fat is an ideal dripping and is especially good for cooking roast potatoes in.

Poultry stock makes a tasty base for many soups and sauces and is lighter than a meat stock. Ideal for poultry and vegetable-based dishes (except for vegetarians).

Suitable for: Leftover poultry carcass, scraps of poultry meat; leftover raw or cooked vegetables.

Ingredients

- 1 chicken or turkey carcass (preferably with giblets but these are not always available)
- 2 rashers bacon (optional)
- 2 onions, cut into quarters
- 2 carrots, cut into quarters
- Water (enough to cover the carcass in the saucepan)
- Salt
- 8 peppercorns
- Bouquet Garni or a pinch of thyme, rosemary, tarragon and parsley

Method:

❶ Fry the chopped up bacon, if using, in a big saucepan for 2 minutes.
❷ Add the carcass and all the other ingredients.
❸ Bring the stock to the boil over a high heat. Then reduce the heat and let the stock simmer gently for 2-3 hours.
❹ When the stock has cooled a little bit, strain it through a sieve.
❺ Leave in a cool place until the fat has formed a hard layer on the top.
❻ Spoon the fat off the top and store stock in the fridge, or freeze in a plastic container.

75

Basic Stock
Meat

⏱ 10 ⏱ 120-180

This tends to be used for stews, meat-based pies and casseroles as it has a stronger flavour than poultry stock.

Suitable for: Meat bones, scraps of meat; leftover vegetables.

Method

❶ Put all the ingredients in the pan and bring the stock to the boil.
❷ Skim off any scum on the surface.
❸ Cover and simmer for 2-3 hours.
❹ Sieve the stock and leave to cool.
❺ Leave in a cool place until the fat has formed a hard layer on the top.
❻ Spoon the fat off the top and store stock in the fridge, or freeze in a plastic container.

Ingredients

- Stripped carcass of a lamb or beef joint or pre-roasted marrow bones or neck of lamb or oxtail
- Carrots
- 2 onions cut into quarters
- Celery, parsnip (optional)
- Seasoning (bay leaf, parsley, thyme, salt, peppercorns)
- Water

76

Basic Stock
Fish

⏲ 10 ⏲ 45

An essential base for really tasty fish soups or fish pie.

Suitable for: Fish bones and heads.

Method

① Put all the ingredients in a large pan and season well with salt and pepper.
② Bring stock to the boil, skim off any scum from the surface, cover and simmer for 30-45 minutes.
③ Strain through fine sieve and cool.
④ Fish stock can be frozen but should not be kept in the fridge for more than 48 hours before using.

Ingredients

- 250g fish bones, with heads
- 1 onion, cut in quarters
- Handful of mushrooms, with peel and stalks
- Pinch of parsley
- Pinch of thyme
- Bay leaf
- A squeeze of lemon juice
- 1 pint water
- ½ pint white wine (optional)
- Salt and pepper

Basic Stock
Vegetable

⏱ 10 ⏱ 90

This stock can be used for any kind or soup or sauce, but especially vegetable-based ones. Vegetable stock is great for making dishes such as risotto, as the flavours from the stock are absorbed by the rice as it cooks.

Suitable for: Raw vegetables.

Ingredients

- 1 onion cut in quarters
- 4-5 of either/combination of carrots, parsnips, swede or mushrooms
- 1 leek, chopped
- Chopped celery (optional}
- Fresh parsley or a pinch of dry parsley
- Salt and pepper
- 3-4 pints water

Method

❶ Put all the ingredients in a large saucepan, bring to the boil and simmer for 1½ hours.
❷ Sieve and allow liquid to cool.
❸ Store in the fridge or freeze.

Basic Recipes: sweet

that can be adapted for different leftovers

Ingredients

Basic sponge cake:

- 200g soft butter or margarine
- 200g caster sugar
- 3 eggs
- 200g self-raising flour
- 1 heaped teaspoon baking powder

Plus any other ingredients of your choice.

Basic Cake Mix

⏱ 15-40 ⏱ 10-80

A good many leftovers can be used up in a cake mixture – whether made into a conventional cake, muffins or party cakes.

What can go in it?

A sponge cake mix can be jazzed up using a variety of **fruits**, **vegetables**, **nuts** and **dried fruit**, **coffee** or **chocolate**. Fruit can either be used in the cake itself or in the filling, mixed with **whipped cream** or **butter icing**, or as decoration on the top of the cake.

Suitable for: Raw apples, bananas, blackcurrants, blueberries, pears, cooked rhubarb; chocolate, coffee granules; raw carrot, raw courgette; lemon or orange juice and zest; nuts; raisins.

Method

1. Preheat the oven to 180°C/350°F/gas mark 4. Use 150°C/300°F/gas mark 2 for carrot cake.
2. Grease two 8 inch round cake tins, or prepare muffin cases on a baking tray.
3. Combine butter and sugar in a food processor until smooth. Add the eggs one at a time and continue blending. Sift the flour and baking powder into the mixture and blend in.
4. Mix in any other ingredients.
5. Divide the mixture evenly between the two cake tins or the muffin cases.
6. For a basic sponge cake, bake in the oven for 20 mins. For muffins, bake for 10-15 minutes. For carrot cake bake for 1 hour 20 minutes and for apple or pear cake bake for 1 hour.
7. Remove from the oven and pass a skewer through the middle of the cake. When the cake is ready, the skewer should come out clean. If not, bake for another 5 minutes.
8. Take out of the oven and cool on a cooling rack.
9. Decorate as required.

Fillings and toppings

A sponge cake can be filled and topped with a number of different ingredients including jam, whipped cream or butter icing.

Basic butter icing

Use half butter/margarine to icing sugar. For a 20cm diameter cake use 150g butter and 300g icing sugar. Beat the ingredients together and add flavouring such as a few drops of vanilla or coffee essence, or, for a chocolate icing, add 25g of cocoa powder and two tablespoons of boiling water.

For a carrot cake icing

Beat together 125g unsalted butter with 50g icing sugar and 250g cream cheese.

Variations

For carrot cake add
- 2 teaspoon cinnamon
- 1 teaspoon bicarbonate of soda
- 150g carrots, finely grated
- 100g walnuts, chopped
- Zest of 1 orange and 1 lemon
- (Use vegetable oil instead of butter)

For apple or pear cake add
- 450g peeled, chopped and cored apples or pears
- 25g ground almonds
- 1 tablespoon Demerara sugar

Other combinations
- Chocolate and blueberry
- Coffee with pecan and walnut topping
- Courgette and banana
- Lemon and banana
- Plain cake with strawberries and cream filling

Ingredients

- 300 – 400g chopped, cored and peeled fruit
- Sugar (few spoonfuls, more if using cooking apples or sour fruit)
- Jam/honey as an alternative to above
- ½ lemon squeezed

For crumble topping

- 200g plain flour or 200g of a combination of flour and oats, flour and muesli, flour and crumbled biscuits
- 75g butter room temperature
- 75g soft brown or caster sugar

For pastry topping

- 450g shortcrust pastry
- Milk or beaten egg to glaze

Variations

- Apple and pear
- Blackberry and apple
- Plums and rhubarb

Basic Crumble (or Pie)
Fruit

🕐 15 🕐 40

Crumbles are fabulous for winter puddings and are a great way to use up leftover fruit. Crumbles freeze very easily so make them up when the fruit is in season when it is cheap and save them for a cold, winter's day.

What can go in it?

Fruit crumbles can be made up of a combination of fruit if you have odd pieces of fruit leftover.

The crumble mix can be varied: using **muesli** and **oats** combined with flour gives the crumble a real crunch, and **leftover crumbled plain biscuits** are also good. A pastry top can easily be substituted for the crumble to make a fruit pie.

Suitable for: Raw apples, apricots, blackberries, blackcurrants, blueberries, cherries, peaches, pears, plums, raspberries, rhubarb.

Method

❶ Pre-heat oven to 180°C/350°F/gas mark 4.
❷ Layer the fruit into bowl (sprinkle each layer with sugar or dollops of jam/honey). Pour the lemon juice over the fruit.
❸ Put flour and sugar into mixing bowl and rub together with your fingers until it looks like breadcrumbs. Add sugar and combine.
❹ Sprinkle the entire crumble ingredients on top of the fruit and cook in the oven for 40 minutes or until crumble has turned golden brown.
❺ Serve hot with cream, crème fraîche, custard or ice cream (or even melted ice cream).
❻ If you are making a pie, roll out the pastry and lay over the dish, glaze with milk or beaten egg, and cook for 35 minutes at 200°C/400°F/gas mark 6.

Basic Fruit Salad

⏱ 10

Fruit salad is a very good way of using up fruit that may no longer look so attractive whole; peel the fruit, throw away any bruised bits – and use the rest.

What can go in it?

There are any number of combinations of fruit that can be used for a fruit salad; for a really good looking fruit salad, try and add some fruits with a range of colours and decorate with mint or borage. Blueberries, strawberries and raspberries provide great colours. Avoid adding banana until you are about to serve the dish, as it quickly discolours once you have peeled it. Fruit salad does not last more than 2-3 days in the fridge, so keep it either in a sealed container – this will help it last longer.

Suitable for: Raw apples, apricots, bananas, blackberries, blackcurrants, blueberries, grapefruit, grapes, kiwi fruit, lychees, melon, oranges, peaches, pears, pineapple, raspberries, satsumas, strawberries, tangerines.

Ingredients

- Any combination of fruit as available

Method

❶ Peel, core/de-seed and chop all the fruit, except bananas, into bite-sized pieces and mix in a large bowl.

❷ For the juice, either (a) put 200ml of water in a saucepan and add 2 tablespoons of sugar, bring to the boil and stir until all the sugar has melted; allow to cool and add to the fruit in the bowl. Or (b) use the juice from a tin of fruit and add a little water or orange juice. Or (c) use up the remains of any fruit juice from the fridge.

❸ Sprinkle a little lemon juice on the fruit salad as this will help prevent discolouration.

❹ Add bananas if using and serve with cream, crème fraîche or yoghurt.

Basic Pasty
Sweet

Sweet pasties are not as widely eaten as savoury ones, but are delicious. They are a quirky alternative to an individual fruit pie, and great for packed lunches. You can make a combination pasty: savoury one end, and fruit the other.

What can go in it?

Basically any **fruit** that bakes well in the oven can be used and will work well. Try adding a little bit of **cinnamon** to a fruit pasty for extra flavour.

Suitable for: Raw apples, apricots, blackberries, blackcurrants, blueberries, raspberries, peaches, pears, rhubarb.

Ingredients (for 4 pasties)
- 450g shortcrust pastry (p.89)
- Milk/egg for glazing

For the filling (sweet)
- Any fruit (see list above) cored, peeled and chopped into cubes
- 2 tablespoons brown sugar
- 1 teaspoon cinnamon

Variations
- Apple and blackcurrant
- Apricot
- Raspberry and apple
- Rhubarb and ginger
- Puff pastry

Method

❶ Preheat the oven to 180°C/350°F/gas mark 4.

❷ Divide pastry into 4 equal pieces and roll each piece out until it is about ½cm thick and you can cut out a circle from it about 20cm in diameter (using a plate).

❸ In a bowl, mix all the filling ingredients and then divide the filling into 4 and spoon it out across the middle of the pastry circles.

❹ Brush the edges of the circles with milk and then bring up the edges to the centre covering the filling. Carefully, using your thumb and forefingers, crimp the edge to form a sealed crest along the top of the pasty, making sure you have left no holes.

❺ When you have done all 4 pasties, lay them on a baking sheet and chill for 30 minutes.

❻ Glaze with milk or beaten egg if you wish.

❼ Bake in the oven for 20 minutes until the fruit and pastry are cooked through.

Basic Smoothies

 1-2

Smoothies are quick to make and can be a fun and delicious part of children's '5 a day' and you can even hide fruit in there that they usually say they don't like! You can also freeze a smoothie and thaw it out when you want it – allow some space in the container because your smoothie will expand when freezing.

What can go in them?

Smoothies are the most fantastic way of using up **soft fruit** that is beginning to look a little 'weary' or perhaps there is just not enough of it left to go around the whole household. There are numerous combinations that can be tried, but the main ingredient in all smoothies is **banana**; here are a number of examples using, as a base, some of our most popular household fruits. Whatever the combination, try freezing the bananas first for a really creamy smoothie or add some ice cubes when you are blending for a crushed ice smoothie!

Suitable for: Leftover or over-ripe bananas, blackberries, blackcurrants, blueberries, passion fruit, peaches, pears, oranges, raspberries, strawberries.

Method for all smoothies

Put all the ingredients into a blender and blend for about 1 minute.

Pink Banana

Ingredients
- 1 banana
- 1 handful of strawberries or raspberries
- 200ml apple juice

Classic Banana

Ingredients
- 2 large bananas
- 1 ripe peach (stoned and peeled)
- Seeds and pulp of one passion fruit
- 1 teaspoon honey

Rare Pear

Ingredients
- 2 pears (peeled and cored) or one tin of pear halves in fruit juice
- 1 banana
- 150ml orange juice
- A dash of lime or lemon juice

Ruby Red

Ingredients

- 3 large handfuls of raspberries
- 200ml cranberry juice
- 2 bananas
- A dollop of natural or Greek yoghurt

Strawberry Slush

Ingredients

- 2 handfuls of strawberries (stalks removed)
- 1 banana
- Juice of two oranges or 150ml orange juice
- A dollop of natural yoghurt

Appleberry Finn

Ingredients

- 2 handfuls of strawberries
- 200ml apple juice

Black 'n' Blueberry

Ingredients

- 2 handfuls of blueberries
- 2 handfuls of blackcurrants
- 1 teaspoon honey
- 5 ice cubes

Belting Blueberry

Ingredients

- 2 handfuls blueberries
- 150ml orange juice
- 6 fresh strawberries
- 1 banana

Basic Stewed Fruit 10 ⏱ 15

Stewed fruit is a delicious pudding on its own, or as the base of a fruit crumble or pie. Try serving stewed fruit on top of vanilla ice cream or with hot custard. It freezes well so if you have some fruit that needs to be used, stew it and then freeze it for use later, either on its own or with a crumble or pie topping on it.

What can go in it?

Combinations of fruit are delicious so if you have a bit of this and a bit of that, don't be afraid to mix and match!

Suitable for: Raw fruit: apples, apricots, blackberries, blackcurrants, blueberries, peaches, pears, plums, redcurrants, rhubarb.

Method

❶ Put all the ingredients in a wide-bottomed saucepan and bring to the boil.
❷ Turn down the heat and let the fruit simmer for another 10 minutes.
❸ Take off the heat and allow to cool.
❹ Remove the cinnamon stick, vanilla pod and clove using a slotted spoon.
❺ Serve or, if using in a crumble, see Fruit Crumble (p.82) for the topping.

Ingredients

- 500g fruit (cored, peeled or de-seeded and chopped/quartered as necessary)
- 3-4 tablespoons sugar (the amounts will vary according to the type of fruit you use)
- Lemon peel
- Cloves (optional)
- Cinnamon stick (optional)
- 1 vanilla pod (optional)
- Water

Variations

- Add a topping – either crumble or shortcrust pastry
- Use wine instead of water e.g. pears in red wine
- Apple and blackberry
- Pear and apricot
- Rhubarb and plum

Basic Shortcrust Pastry

⏱ 10-30

Whilst you can buy pre-made pastry, it is easy – and cheaper – to make your own. Short-crust pastry can be used in fruit and vegetable pies and pasties, quiches, flans and tarts. Once made, pastry can be frozen or stored in the fridge for about 3-4 days, although don't store it for any longer as it tends to become rather crumbly. It is extremely important to use cold butter. If the butter (or butter and lard mixture) becomes warm it coats more flour grains than it should, which means the flour is unable to absorb enough water and the pastry will crumble and be difficult to roll out. Likewise, don't overdo it when you are combining the fat with the flour, just rub it in enough to make the mixture crumbly. While you are doing it, try and lift the flour mixture up into the air allowing as much air as possible into the mixture.

Don't skimp on the process by not resting the dough in the fridge for at least 30 minutes – pastry contains gluten which, in time, has an elasticity which is important when you roll it out as it prevents the dough from cracking.

Makes enough pastry to line a 25cm round quiche dish or a 25-30cm oval dish.

Method

❶ Put the flour and salt in a bowl (you can sift it but I don't usually bother) and dice up the butter into the mixture. Using your fingers, rub the butter and flour together until it looks like breadcrumbs.

❷ Add the cold water, a little at a time, and mix in well until the mixture can form a ball without being too sticky. Tip the dough out onto a floured surface and gently knead the pastry until you have a smooth firm ball. Don't overdo it or you will end up with very hard pastry. Put in a plastic bag in the fridge for at least 30 minutes.

❸ To prepare, roll it out on a floured work surface so that it is just larger than the dish it is to cover or fill.

Ingredients

- 250g plain flour
- 150g unsalted butter (or 75g butter and 75g lard)
- Pinch of salt
- 3-4 tablespoons cold water

Variations

Add grated cheese for a savoury dish.

Basic Recipes: sweet

Individual Recipes: savoury

Other fillings

- Baked beans
- Chopped bacon
- Chopped ham
- Grated cheese
- Sour cream

Baked Potato Fillings

The possibilities for baked potato fillings are endless which makes a baked potato such a wonderful platform for using up leftovers. Make sure the potato is cooked all the way through and nice and crispy on the outside. Some **potatoes** are more suited to baking than others, either because of their size, water content, skin type or flesh structure; they include Maris Piper, King Edward and Desirée but if you want to try something a bit different, look for Duke of York, Nadine or Romano.

You could also experiment by baking a **sweet potato** instead, which roasts beautifully and is especially good with melted butter inside. Here are just a few suggestions for fillings (quantities per potato, adjust according to required amounts).

Leftovers used

Old or hard cheese, cooked chicken, cranberry sauce, curry or tomato sauce, leftover stew, cooked roasted vegetables. Cooking times for baked potatoes vary from 1 hour to 1½ hours depending on the size of the potato. They should be cooked on the top shelf of the oven at 200°C/400°F/gas mark 6.

Brie with Cranberry Sauce

🕐 10

❶ Scoop out the middle of the baked potato and mix it with 50-70g soft brie (depending on the size of the potato) and a dessertspoonful of cranberry sauce.

❷ Put the mixture back in the potato and place under a hot grill for 5 minutes until it goes crispy on top.

Chicken Mayonnaise with Sweet Corn

🕐 5

❶ Mix 50g of cooked chicken with 1 tablespoon mayonnaise and a small tin of sweet corn.

❷ Add black pepper to taste and a sprinkling of grated cheese on top.

Curried chicken

 5

❶ Mix 50g of cooked chicken with 1 tablespoon of mayonnaise and a pinch of curry powder.
❷ Add a small handful of raisins or sliced up grapes.

Crème fraîche/natural yoghurt with red onion and red pepper

 10

❶ Fry half a chopped red onion and half a red pepper until soft.
❷ Mix the last scrapings of a pot of crème fraîche or natural yoghurt into the mixture.

Curry/stew/bolognaise sauce

 10

❶ Heat up the leftover curry, bolognaise sauce or stew in a saucepan.
❷ If the leftovers are a little dry, add a spoonful of crème fraîche, cream or natural yoghurt and stir in well.

Roasted vegetables

 10

❶ Reheat the roasted vegetables in a saucepan, stirring all the time.
❷ Serve with lots of black pepper and grated Parmesan cheese (optional).

Tuna and tomato sauce

7

❶ Use up any tomato pasta sauce by adding a tin of tuna and mixing well.
❷ Heat well and serve.

Braised Beef with Winter Vegetables ⏱ 15 ⏱ 165

Despite rising food costs, it is still possible to produce a family meal that does not cost the earth by being a little more enterprising with the choice of meat you cook. For beef, a joint of topside or silverside is expensive but for this recipe I suggest using brisket or even shin of beef, which may not be readily on offer in supermarkets but will be available from a butcher.

These cuts need to be cooked slowly for a long time, which makes them perfect for this recipe as the leftover raw winter **vegetables** have ample time to soak in the delicious flavours from the beef and its juices. The leftovers are fabulous on a baked potato.

Suitable for six people.

Leftovers used

Raw winter vegetables: carrots, leeks, onions, parsnips, swede, sweet potato, turnip.

Method

❶ Preheat the oven to 150°/300°F/gas mark 2.

❷ Put the flour in a flat dish, season with salt and pepper and roll the meat in it until it is coated in the flour. Keep the flour to use later.

❸ Heat the oil in a heavy lidded casserole dish. When the oil is really hot, brown the meat all over for a few minutes. Remove with a slotted spoon onto a plate.

❹ Using the same casserole, fry the onion and garlic in the oil (you may have to add a little more oil) for about 3 minutes until soft. Add the remaining vegetables and mixed herbs and stir them around in the oil for about 3 minutes.

❺ Add about a spoonful of the seasoned flour (from stage 2) to the vegetables and stir it in.

❻ Stir in the wine and stock and allow to bubble for about 2 minutes until the sauce has reduced by about half. Season with salt and pepper.

❼ Return the meat to the pot, arranging the vegetables around it, put the lid on and transfer to the oven.

❽ For brisket or shin cook for at least 50 minutes per kilo plus 30 minutes. For this 2kg piece of brisket, cook for a minimum of 2 hours and 10 minutes – 2½ hours is ideal.

Ingredients

- 2kg rolled brisket of beef, or shin of beef cut into large chunks
- Flour for coating the meat
- A generous slug of vegetable oil
- 2 onions, quartered
- 2 cloves garlic
- 4 carrots, roughly chopped
- Selection of leeks, parsnips, sweet potato, swede, turnip, roughly chopped
- 1 glass red wine
- 250ml beef stock
- 1 teaspoon mixed herbs
- Salt and pepper

Bubble and Squeak

⏱ 5 ⏱ 15

Possibly the ultimate leftover dish, this is loved universally by young and old and is a fantastic Sunday-evening-in-front-of-the-telly dish! Alternatively, serve it with a fried or poached egg on top for a cooked breakfast with a difference.

You can add just about any leftover cooked **vegetables** to this dish, but mashed or grated **potato** is essential.

To really add flavour to this recipe, cook the bacon in lard or dripping (the fat from meat), which you can collect when you do a roast joint. Dripping can be kept in a covered container in the fridge for up to two weeks.

If you are vegetarian, omit bacon from the recipe and use sunflower oil for frying instead of dripping/lard.

Leftovers used

Cooked vegetables: broccoli, Brussels sprouts, cabbage, greens, sweet corn.

Method

1. Fry the onion or leek in the dripping or butter in a non-stick frying pan for about 3 minutes until soft.
2. Add the bacon and fry until nicely browned.
3. Meanwhile mash together the veggies and potato and season.
4. Add the bacon and onions or leek to the potato and mix it all in well.
5. Transfer it back to the frying pan, flatten into a pancake shape using the back of a wooden spoon and fry the mixture in the oil for about 4 minutes on each side, until it is crispy and golden brown. Make sure you turn it over very carefully using a fish slice to prevent it falling apart.
6. Turn it out onto warm plate and divide up into wedges.

Ingredients

· 400g of mash
· 300g (ish) of cooked cabbage/greens/Brussels sprouts
· 1 leek or small onion, chopped
· 4 rashers of chopped streaky bacon
· 1 small tin sweet corn or the remains of a tin (optional)
· 25g dripping or butter

Individual Recipes: savoury

Butternut Squash Coconut Curry

🕐 10 🕐 20

This curry is very easy to make and relatively quick. I love this dish served with basmati rice and a dollop of natural **yoghurt** or lassi (Indian yoghurt), but it is also delicious just on its own.

Just about any combination of **vegetables** is possible but things like **sweet potato** and **swede** are great for absorbing the flavours from the coconut milk, lemongrass and chilli, so they are an important ingredient.

Leftovers used

Raw or cooked baby corn, broccoli, cauliflower, carrots, green or runner beans, squash, swede, potatoes, peas, sweet potato.

Method

❶ Put onion, garlic, ginger, lemongrass, chilli, turmeric, salt, lime juice and oil in a blender/food processor and purée until it makes a smooth paste.

❷ Peel the butternut squash. Chop off the stalk and flower end. Chop in half and use a spoon to remove the seeds. Chop into ½ inch cubes.

❸ Prepare the other raw vegetables by chopping into rough chunks.

❹ Put the paste into a large pan or wok and fry gently, stirring, for 2 minutes. If you are using uncooked chicken or prawns, then add these now and cook in the paste for about 3 minutes, coating them well in the spices.

❺ Add the raw vegetables and stir, to coat them in the paste.

❻ Add the coconut milk and mix well.

❼ Cook gently, uncovered, for 10-15 minutes, until the vegetables are tender and the sauce has thickened. Stir occasionally, to prevent burning and uneven cooking. Add more water if the sauce gets too dry before the vegetables are cooked.

❽ If using cooked vegetables, add them to the pan when you have about 5 minutes remaining and mix well to ensure they warm through.

❾ Serve on its own or with basmati rice.

Ingredients

- 2 cloves of garlic
- 1 thumbnail-size piece of fresh root ginger, peeled and roughly chopped
- 1 inch piece of lemongrass (optional)
- 1 fresh chilli
- ½ teaspoon ground turmeric
- ¼ teaspoon salt
- Juice of 1 lime
- 30ml oil (sesame oil is best, but sunflower oil or olive oil is fine)
- 1 butternut squash
- 1 medium onion, peeled and roughly chopped
- 500g of any of the above vegetables, chopped
- 400g tin coconut milk

Variations

- Prawn or chicken curry

Caramelised Onion and Tomato Tart

⏱ 30-60 ⏱ 70

Sometimes I find that I have loads of **onions** in my vegetable rack (a result of several 'Groundhog Day' moments when I go shopping and repeatedly buy more onions!) and so onion and tomato tart is such a good way of wading through a few of them!

Ideally, use red onions as they have such a fabulous flavour, but really tasty white onions will be fine. You can either make one big onion tart or, if you have some **pastry** left over from making a pie or quiche, then you can make small, individual tarts.

You will need a 25cm flan dish or shallow rectangular baking tray

Leftovers used

Raw onions; leftover pastry; soft tomatoes.

Method

❶ Preheat the oven to 190°C/375°F/gas mark 5.

❷ Melt the butter in a frying pan over a low heat. Add the onions and sugar and cook slowly for about ½ hour, making sure the onions don't burn but just caramelise in the sugar.

❸ Grease the flan dish or baking tray, roll out the shortcrust pastry so it is a little bigger than the dish or tray, and line the dish or tray with the pastry. Prick the base a number of times with a fork – this will prevent the pastry rising on the base – and cook in the oven for about 15 minutes until the pastry just turns light brown.

❹ Take out of the oven and line the bottom of the pastry with the caramelised onions.

❺ Lay the sliced tomatoes over the onions and then sprinkle the fresh or dried basil on top of the tomatoes. Season with salt and pepper.

❻ Place back in the oven and cook for another 20 minutes until the tomatoes are cooked.

❼ Serve with some grated Parmesan on top.

Ingredients

- 4 medium-sized onions, sliced
- A large knob of butter
- 1 tablespoon Demerara or soft brown sugar
- 4 large tomatoes, sliced
- 2 tablespoons fresh basil or 1 dessertspoon dried basil
- Salt and pepper
- Parmesan cheese

For the pastry

- 450g shortcrust pastry

Individual Recipes: savoury

97

Carrot and Cumin Soup 10 50

This is a wonderful winter warmer and can be made whenever you have some **carrots** or **celery** left in the vegetable rack. You only need two or three carrots to make enough for two people – this recipe is for four to six people.

Don't worry if your carrots have gone a little wrinkly or, as sometimes happens, especially with carrots that have been refrigerated, they are slightly black on the outside – if you peel them well the carrot will still be perfectly alright to use and will not have lost any flavour or goodness.

This soup also freezes well so make the soup when you have spare carrots and freeze it for another occasion.

Like all good soups, a really good stock will make it even more delicious but you can use good stock cubes if you don't have any homemade stock.

Ingredients

- 1 tablespoon olive oil
- 25g butter
- 1 medium onion, chopped
- 1 garlic clove, crushed
- 2 sticks of celery, chopped
- 1 dessertspoon ground cumin
- 500g carrots, sliced
- 700ml vegetable stock
- Black pepper to taste
- Fresh coriander to garnish

Leftovers used

Raw carrots; celery.

Method

1. Heat the oil and butter in a large saucepan, add the onion, garlic and celery and cook over a medium heat for about 5 minutes, until soft.
2. Add the cumin and mix in for about 1 minute.
3. Add the carrots, stock and some black pepper and mix in well.
4. Increase the heat so that the soup comes to the boil and then simmer with a lid on for about 30 minutes or until the vegetables are softened. Stir occasionally.
5. Allow the soup to cool for about 10 minutes and then transfer to a blender or food processor. Purée until the soup is smooth – this is a soup that is best without lumps.
6. Gently reheat the soup when you want to serve it, with a little coriander leaf to garnish – or allow to cool and freeze.

Cheese Soufflé

🕐 20 🕐 40

If you haven't cooked a soufflé before, don't try out your first one on a dinner party for 10 people – try it out first. I always keep the 'dog ends' of fresh **Parmesan** – the bits that have gone rather hard at the end – and save them up in my 'leftovers' shelf in the door of the fridge.

If you are lucky enough to have lovely free range eggs (or have access to them) then try to use them here as the colour of soufflé they produce is stunning! Soufflé is delicious eaten on its own or with a slice of fresh bread (to soak up the gooey bits).

You will need a 1½ pint soufflé dish.

Leftovers used

Bits of fresh Parmesan or Gruyère; the remains of a packet of grated Parmesan.

Method:

❶ Preheat the oven to 200°C/400°F/gas mark 6.
❷ Melt the butter in a saucepan, add the flour and mix well to remove any lumps.
❸ Add the warm milk and stir in to make a smooth, white sauce. Allow this to cook, on a very low heat, for about 10 minutes, stirring frequently.
❹ Add the grated cheese and then, very slowly add the beaten egg yolks, adding a little at a time and stirring constantly.
❺ Take off the heat and add a pinch of Cayenne pepper and salt and pepper to taste and mix well.
❻ Put the mixture to one side and, if possible, leave for about an hour.
❼ In a bowl, whisk the egg whites until they can form stiff peaks and the mixture is really light and fluffy.
❽ Very gently fold the egg yolk mixture into the egg whites, adding a little at a time.
❾ Pour the mixture into the soufflé dish, trying not to lose any air from the mixture. Using a palette knife, score a circle around the top of the mixture – this will give it a cottage loaf look when it rises.
❿ Place in the oven and cook for approximately 25 minutes (this will depend very much on your dish and how carefully you have folded the egg whites in). The soufflé will be ready when it has risen nicely and turned slightly brown on the top. When ready, serve immediately with a slice of really fresh bread.

Ingredients

- 1 tablespoon flour
- 25g butter
- ½ pint of warm milk
- 50g finely grated Parmesan or 25g each of Parmesan and Gruyère
- 4 large egg yolks, well beaten
- Cayenne pepper
- Salt and pepper to taste
- 5 large egg whites

Individual Recipes: savoury

Cheesy Chicken Breasts 5 30

We use cream **cheese** in our house quite a bit but there are often times when I have used half a tub and the remainder is on the verge of going off and needs eating quickly. This is just one idea for using up the leftovers and is always a favourite with our family.

This dish is especially nice served in summer with new potatoes and roasted vegetables. I like to put sun dried tomatoes inside the chicken breasts but other ideas include adding some finely chopped chilli or diced, fried **bacon** or pancetta.

You will need some cocktail sticks and aluminium foil.

Ingredients

- 4 chicken breasts
- Approximately ½ tub of cream cheese (although the more the better)
- Sun dried tomatoes (optional)
- 3 slices of bacon or pancetta, fried and chopped (optional)
- 3 small sprigs of fresh thyme
- Salt and pepper to taste

Leftovers used

Remains of a tub of cream cheese; cooked or raw bacon or pancetta.

Method

1. Flatten out the chicken breasts on a chopping board and paste the cream cheese onto one side of the breasts.
2. Add the sun dried tomatoes and cooked bacon or pancetta (if using).
3. Roll the chicken breasts up so that the cream cheese is on the inside.
4. Push one cocktail stick through the middle of each chicken breast so that it holds the meat in place.
5. Line a baking tray with a piece of aluminium foil. Place the chicken breasts on the foil, lay the sprigs of thyme on top and then cover with another layer of foil. Fold the edges of the foil over each other so that any juices from the chicken are retained within the foil pocket.
6. Bake in the oven for approximately 25-30 minutes, until the chicken is cooked but still moist.
7. Remove the foil and serve (with the cocktail stick still in place) with new potatoes and roasted vegetables or green salad.

Cheesy Leeks and Ham

⏱ 10 ⏱ 15

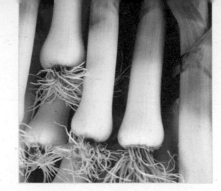

This is such a simple recipe and one which children will enjoy as much as grown ups. If you have one leek left in the vegetable rack you can still make a filling meal for one. The rule of thumb is that you need one good-sized leek per person.

If your **leeks** are rather dry on the outside just remove the dried outer layers and the vegetable underneath will still be tasty.

This recipe is a good one to keep up your sleeve at Christmas time when there may be some **ham** or **gammon** left over and leeks are at a reasonable price. It's also an ideal way to use up any 'ends' of **cheese** – again, ideal after Christmas, although I don't recommend using too much stilton unless you like very rich food!

Leftovers used

Hard cheese, cooked ham, raw leeks.

Method

❶ Steam the leeks for about 6 minutes, so they are still crunchy.

❷ Let the leeks cool for a few minutes and then wrap a slice of ham around each half of leek and lay the leeks in a flat-bottomed, ovenproof dish.

❸ Meanwhile, make a cheese sauce by melting the butter in a saucepan. Add the flour and stir well. Add the milk, or milk and vegetable water, a bit at a time, stirring in constantly, until it makes a thickish sauce. Keep adding liquid until the sauce is the required thickness. Add about ⅔ of the cheese, plus mustard or Cayenne pepper and salt and pepper and stir in until it has melted into the sauce.

❹ Pour the sauce over the leeks and sprinkle the remaining cheese over the top.

❺ Place under a hot grill for 5-10 minutes until the cheese has browned on the top.

Ingredients

- One leek per person, cut in half widthways
- 1 slice of ham per half leek

For the sauce (for 4 people)

- 50g butter
- 1 tablespoon flour
- 200ml milk (or mixture of milk and vegetable water from cooking leeks)
- 150g Cheddar or Gruyère cheese, grated
- 1 teaspoon mustard (optional)
- Pinch Cayenne pepper (optional)
- Salt and pepper

Individual Recipes: savoury

Ingredients

- 500g chicken or turkey meat
- 200g broccoli or leeks (chopped into small pieces) or peas
- 1 small tin sweet corn (optional)
- 50g butter
- 2 tablespoons plain flour
- 250ml milk/vegetable water
- 1 tablespoon mayonnaise
- 1 tablespoon lemon/lime juice
- 200g grated cheese
- Salt & pepper
- 1 packet of crisps/ 3 tablespoons stale bread

Chicken Crunch

 15 25

My whole inspiration for compiling a book about using up leftovers came from this one recipe: you can make a chicken last for five meals and this is one of the many ideas for using up the remains of a roast chicken.

This recipe is equally good using turkey – so it's great for post-Christmas desperation – but whichever poultry you use, if you strip the meat from the carcass when the bird is still warm the meat comes away from the bones more easily.

This is a great recipe for children as they love the cheesy sauce and crispy topping and it's also useful for using up any leftover raw vegetables, such as broccoli and leeks, as well as any opened packets of crisps that have gone slightly stale.

Leftovers used

Cooked chicken or turkey; cooked or raw broccoli, leeks, peas, sweet corn; hard cheese; stale bread (breadcrumbs).

Method

1. Pre-heat the oven at 200°C/400°F/gas mark 6.
2. Boil or steam any raw vegetables for about 5 minutes so they are still crunchy, keeping the water from the pan to use later in the sauce if you wish.
3. Put the chicken and cooked vegetables into a flat-bottomed ovenproof dish and add the drained sweet corn (if using).
4. Melt the butter in a saucepan and blend in the flour.
5. Gradually blend in the milk, stirring constantly over a medium heat until the sauce becomes thick and smooth. Use broccoli water instead of some/all of the milk if you wish.
6. When you have a reasonably thick sauce, add the mayonnaise, lemon/lime juice and half the grated cheese and stir in well. Add salt and pepper to taste.
7. Pour the sauce over the chicken and vegetables. Crunch the crisps into small pieces and sprinkle these, or breadcrumbs if using, evenly over the chicken and sauce, followed by the remains of the grated cheese.
8. Bake in the oven for about 20-25 minutes until golden.
9. Serve with rice or potatoes.

Chicken Liver and Wild Mushroom Pâté

⏰ 30

Try and buy a chicken which has the giblets and **livers** with it; the giblets make fantastic stock for the chicken gravy and you can freeze the livers until you have enough to make chicken liver pâté. Be careful not to cook the chicken and then discover the little plastic bag containing the giblets still inside!

A selection of wild mushrooms is ideal for this dish, although ordinary mushrooms will do. Once made, chicken liver pâté should last in the fridge for 5-6 days.

Leftovers used

Uncooked chicken livers.

Method

❶ Trim off any fatty bits from the livers.

❷ In a large frying pan, fry the shallots, pancetta or bacon, garlic and thyme in the olive oil until the shallots are soft and translucent. Remove from the pan, drain on some kitchen paper and transfer to a food processor.

❸ Using the remaining oil in the pan, fry the chicken livers and add them to the food processor, along with any juices and oil from the pan and the brandy. Blend until the pâté is reasonably smooth.

❹ Meanwhile, soak the wild mushrooms in some boiling water for a few minutes, drain, pat dry and roughly chop them.

❺ Fry the mushrooms in 25g of the butter over a medium heat for about 4 minutes until soft.

❻ Add the mushrooms to the pâté and blend them in well.

❼ Transfer the pâté into individual ramekin dishes or a small loaf tin.

❽ Melt the remaining butter in a saucepan and pour over the pâté, either in the individual dishes or the loaf tin. Decorate with a sprig of thyme and transfer to the fridge to chill.

❾ Serve on bruschetta or thinly sliced toast.

Ingredients

- 3 rashers of pancetta or smoked bacon, chopped
- 2 shallots, finely chopped
- Olive oil for cooking
- A sprig of thyme leaves, chopped
- 1 clove garlic
- 600g chicken livers
- 1 tablespoon sweet sherry or brandy
- 100g unsalted butter
- Black pepper
- 30g wild mushrooms (mixed if possible)

Individual Recipes: savoury

Chicken Spring Rolls

 30 **10**

There is quite a long list of ingredients, but don't be put off as this is an easy recipe!

Naturally, you don't need to include chicken in the recipe – a solely vegetable spring roll is delicious. Try adding some shredded cabbage, which is tasty combined with the soy sauce.

Leftovers used

Cooked chicken; raw carrots, bean sprouts; cooked cabbage, carrots or peas.

Makes 12 spring rolls.

Method

1. Shred the chicken meat into small pieces.
2. In a wok or frying pan, heat the sesame oil over a high heat. Add the garlic, ginger, mushrooms, raw cabbage, carrot, bean sprouts and peas and cook for 2 minutes.
3. Add the chicken and any cooked vegetables and stir in for a couple of minutes to heat through.
4. Stir in the soy sauce and Chinese five spice and mix the ingredients well.
5. Lay a spring roll wrap on a work surface with one point facing towards you. Spoon 2 tablespoons of the filling near the corner closest to you and fold up to enclose the filling. Fold in the two sides and brush the top seam of the wrap with the beaten egg. Continue rolling up.
6. If using filo pastry: lay one sheet in front of you, spoon 2 tablespoons of the filling at one end and roll it up, tucking in the sides neatly to make a parcel. Immediately, roll the roll in a second sheet of filo pastry.
7. Pour the vegetable oil into the wok and heat over a very high heat. When the oil is really hot, add the spring rolls and cook for about 2 minutes, turning to cook on all sides until the wrap is crisp.
8. Drain well on kitchen paper and serve hot or cold with sweet chilli sauce.

Individual Recipes: savoury

Ingredients

- 12 spring roll wraps or 24 sheets filo pastry
- 1 tablespoon sesame oil
- About 150-200g cooked chicken meat
- 1 teaspoon chilli powder or 1 fresh chilli de-seeded and chopped
- 1 tablespoon soy sauce
- 1 tablespoon Chinese five spice
- Handful Chinese mushrooms (soaked for 20 minutes and drained)
- 1 clove garlic
- ½ tablespoon grated ginger
- About 75g bean sprouts
- 1 carrot, grated (cooked or raw)
- Shredded cabbage (cooked or raw) (optional)
- Handful frozen or cooked peas (optional)
- 1 egg, beaten
- Vegetable oil for frying

For serving

- Sweet chilli sauce

Chilli con Carne

 10 30

Although chilli con carne is normally made using raw beef, there is no reason why cooked, minced beef cannot be used, so long as the meat has not dried out too much. Purists might say that the meat does not have the opportunity to absorb the flavours while it is cooking but I would argue that the beef has already absorbed its own flavours from when it was first cooked.

If you are using leftover beef from a joint, the secret to keeping the beef moist is to mince it only when you are about to use it – keep it on the bone (or in one piece) for as long as possible before using so that less of the meat is exposed to the air. Once minced the meat must be kept in an airtight container in the fridge, or it can be frozen.

If you do not have enough cooked beef leftover, bulk out the recipe with either more tinned kidney beans or a tin of flageolet, cannelloni or haricot beans.

This recipe is for a medium hot chilli, but it can be altered depending on how spicy you like your food.

Leftovers used

Cooked, minced or diced beef.

Method

1. Heat the oil in a deep frying pan, add the onions and cook for 3-4 minutes until golden.
2. Add the garlic, peppers and fresh chillies or chilli powder and cook for another 2 minutes.
3. Add the tinned tomatoes and the kidney beans (and any other beans you may be using as a meat substitute) and cover the contents with stock.
4. Add the bay leaves and simmer for 30 minutes.
5. After 30 minutes add the cooked minced meat and continue to simmer for another 10 minutes.
6. Serve with baked potatoes or rice with a dollop of sour cream if available and a green salad on the side.

Ingredients

- 400-500g cooked beef, either minced or in chunks
- 1 large onion, chopped
- 1 clove of garlic, crushed
- 400g tin of kidney beans, drained
- ½ a teaspoon chilli powder or 1 fresh chilli, de-seeded and chopped
- 1-2 peppers, de-seeded and chopped
- 400g tin chopped tomatoes
- 2 bay leaves
- 200ml stock or water
- 1 tablespoon sunflower oil, salt and pepper

Chinese Pork with Water Chestnuts

⏱ 15 ⏱ 10

In my opinion, unlike beef, lamb or chicken, cold pork is not nearly as tasty as when it is hot and so we tend to have to be a bit more inventive when it comes to using up the leftovers. This is a very mild Chinese fried rice dish which not only uses up leftover pork but also cold, cooked rice.

As with other cold, cooked meat, it is essential to prevent it from drying out – either keep the cold meat on the bone or in one piece, until you need to use it. If you want to freeze roast pork, slice or cut it up and lay the single pieces on a layer of greaseproof paper, then cover with another layer so that each portion can be taken out of the freezer individually when needed.

Leftovers used

Cooked pork; cooked rice.

Ingredients

- 4 tablespoons sesame oil
- 1 clove garlic
- 1 small onion, diced
- A handful of fresh mushrooms, sliced
- 1 small tin of water chestnuts, sliced
- 100g frozen peas (or leftover cooked peas)
- 450g cold, cooked rice, or equivalent uncooked rice
- 300g cooked pork, diced
- 2 tablespoon soy sauce
- 2 eggs, beaten

Method

1. If you are using uncooked rice, cook it, drain and put to one side.
2. Heat 2 tablespoons of the oil in a frying pan or wok over a high heat. When hot, add the onion and garlic and stir-fry for 2 minutes.
3. Add the mushrooms and water chestnuts and stir-fry for 2 more minutes.
4. Add the rice and peas and stir until the rice is warmed through. Add the pork and soy sauce and continue stirring the mixture for another 3 minutes.
5. Push the rice mixture to one side of the pan. Add the remaining oil to the pan and, when hot, add the beaten eggs.
6. When the eggs begin to set, combine them with the rice, pork and vegetables. Stir well and serve.

Coronation Turkey

⏱ 10

Coronation Chicken was invented by Constance Spry and first served at the Queen's Coronation lunch in 1953. Since then it has become a classic, most notably served at summer weddings and al fresco lunches and lots of people have developed their own variations of the original Spry recipe.

Although this recipe uses turkey, it is the sauce, as much as the quality and type of poultry you use, that is important. Over the years I have tried a number of different variations and this one is undoubtedly my favourite although I don't think I have ever produced two exactly the same, so don't be afraid to play around with the quantities to suit your own taste.

Coronation turkey is a very useful variation as it offers yet another string to your bow for that after-Christmas period when leftovers start taking over your kitchen.

Leftovers used

Cooked turkey.

Method

1. Cut or shred the turkey meat into bite-sized pieces.
2. Put the apricots into a blender and blend until there are very few lumps.
3. In a bowl, mix the blended apricot, mango chutney, curry powder, lemon juice, mayonnaise, cream and sultanas. Really mix this well before adding black pepper to taste.
4. Add the turkey meat and stir in until it is coated in the sauce.
5. Serve with a generous garnish of watercress.

Ingredients

- 400-500g of cooked turkey
- 5 dried apricots
- 2 tablespoons mango chutney
- 1 dessertspoon curry powder
- Juice of half a lemon
- 3 tablespoons mayonnaise
- 100ml whipping or single cream
- Black pepper to taste
- 150g sultanas (optional)
- Watercress to garnish

Variations

- Coronation chicken

Individual Recipes: savoury

Courgette and Pasta Bake

⏱ 10 ⏱ 30

This is a really quick and easy recipe that uses up that lone **courgette**. Although this recipe will serve 4 people and I have therefore used 3 courgettes, one medium to large courgette will do for 2 people.

You might want to add other ingredients as well, such as sliced and fried **chorizo** or pancetta or cooked **ham**, but it is good just on its own with lots of **Parmesan** on top.

This is also a useful recipe if you've made too much **pasta**.

Leftovers used

Raw courgettes; cooked pasta e.g. fettuccine or tagliatelle.

Method

1 Heat the oil and butter in a frying pan or large saucepan. Add the courgettes, onion, garlic and mushrooms and cook over a gentle heat for about 5 minutes.
2 Stir in the tomatoes, herbs, turmeric and sherry (if using).
3 Bring to the boil and then turn it down and simmer for 5 minutes.
4 Add the cream and let it simmer for another 15-20 minutes.
5 If using uncooked fettuccine, cook it according to the instructions, or, if using cooked pasta, then run some boiling water through it whilst teasing it with a fork, to remove any stickiness.
6 Serve the courgette sauce on top of the fettuccine with lots of Parmesan.

Ingredients

- 2 tablespoons olive oil
- Knob of butter
- 250g of fettuccine or other pasta
- 1 teaspoon turmeric
- ½ teaspoon dried basil
- 2 garlic cloves, crushed
- ½ teaspoon dried mint
- 150g mushrooms, sliced
- 300ml double cream
- 5 tablespoons sherry (optional)
- 3 medium-sized courgettes (or 4 small courgettes), diced
- 400g tin chopped tomatoes
- Grated Parmesan

Eggs over Peppers and Tomatoes

⏱ 10-20 ⏱ 10

This is a fantastic Sunday night supper dish and especially good with really fresh, free-range eggs; their bright orange yolks provide a great contrast with the brightly coloured peppers and tomatoes.

Peppers and tomatoes can often be left in the vegetable rack or bottom drawer of the fridge and this is an ideal recipe for using them up. A combination of yellow and red peppers is ideal but either is delicious and sweet; alternatively, any leftover cooked peppers can be used.

Don't be afraid to use peppers and tomatoes that are a little soft or wrinkly, they will cook in the oven and taste just as good as fresh vegetables.

The recipe here is for 2 people but the quantities are very flexible, depending on what you have available.

Leftovers used

Roast peppers; raw peppers, tomatoes.

Method

❶ For raw peppers, pre-heat the oven to 200°C.

❷ Core and de-seed the pepper and chop into chunks. Cook in a little olive oil in the oven for about 20 minutes until soft and slightly browning. Remove from the oven but don't discard the oil.

❸ Roughly chop the tomato and sauté in a frying pan or skillet, over a high heat, in a tablespoon of olive oil plus any oil from roasting the peppers until soft. Season with salt, pepper and a pinch of basil.

❹ Add the roast peppers, either freshly roasted or leftover, cook for about 2 minutes and then reduce the heat.

❺ Sprinkle over the Parmesan and then break the eggs over the top.

❻ Bake until eggs are done to your liking.

Ingredients

- 1 large pepper (red or yellow), roasted or raw
- 2 large tomatoes, chopped
- Olive oil
- Pinch of basil
- 100g Parmesan, grated
- 4 eggs

Individual Recipes: savoury

Fish Cakes

 15 ⏱ 10

Fish cakes are a wonderful meal to make using leftovers: any grilled or poached **fish** from yesterday along with that cold bowl of mashed **potato** you might have in the fridge and **breadcrumbs** from the freezer. You can even add some leftover cooked **peas** or finely chopped cooked **carrots** or **leeks**.

If you have a pile of mashed potato in the fridge and don't have any fresh fish, then a tin of **tuna** from your store cupboard can swing into action enabling you to rustle up a quick and easy meal.

Make sure your breadcrumbs are reasonably finely processed to make a nice smooth outer surface to your fishcakes, ensuring that they fry evenly all over.

Leftovers used

Cooked fish; cooked mashed potato; cooked vegetables: leeks, peas.

Method

❶ Mash the fish, potatoes, tomato, spring onions, finely chopped cooked vegetables and egg together with a fork.
❷ Season with salt and pepper.
❸ Divide mixture into 8 and shape into patties.
❹ Season the breadcrumbs with salt and pepper and spread them out on a flat plate and roll the fish cakes in the breadcrumbs.
❺ Heat up oil and butter in large frying pan (preferably non-stick) and, when hot, add the fish cakes.
❻ Fry for about 3-4 minutes on each side taking care not to let the butter burn.
❼ Serve immediately. Delicious served with a green salad and sweet chilli sauce.

Ingredients

- 2 tins tuna or 275g of cooked fillet of any fish
- 400g mashed potato
- 2 tomatoes, skins removed and finely chopped (optional)
- 2 spring onions (finely sliced)
- 150g cooked peas, leeks or carrots, finely chopped
- 1 egg
- 8-10 tablespoons breadcrumbs made with stale bread
- 3 tablespoons oil
- 25g butter
- Lemon wedges for serving

Green Pea Soup

🕐 15 🕐 15

There is nothing like the taste of fresh pea soup. If you grow your own peas, you may find they all ripen at once, in which case this recipe may come to your rescue. It can also be used if you've seriously over-catered and have a saucepan of cooked peas left over. Just adjust the quantities to suit the amount of peas that you have.

Raw peas freeze well. You can 'blanch' peas for about 2 minutes in boiling water before freezing or you can lay them out on a tray in the freezer and transfer them to a freezer bag when frozen and of course soup freezes well for later.

Leftovers used

Raw peas or a large amount of cooked peas.

Method

① If using uncooked peas, put the peas with the mint and pea pods in a small amount of salted water and cook until tender.

② Put the cooked peas in a blender and process until smooth (or push through a sieve if you don't have a blender). Combine the purée with the stock or water.

③ Melt the butter or margarine in a saucepan and blend in the flour. Cook for a couple of minutes.

④ Add the puréed peas and stock gradually until fully blended. Season with salt and pepper.

⑤ Bring to the boil and then lower the heat and allow to simmer for about 5 minutes.

⑥ Stir in the milk or cream and warm through.

⑦ Serve with a sprig of fresh mint.

Ingredients

- 400g freshly shelled peas or equivalent cooked peas
- A few young pea pods (optional)
- Sprig of fresh mint
- 1 litre (about 2 pints) of vegetable stock or water
- Salt and pepper
- 25g butter or margarine
- 1 tablespoon flour
- 150ml milk or cream

Individual Recipes: savoury

Guacamole

 10

It is very difficult to buy an avocado that is 'just right', and this is particularly true when buying from a supermarket. They usually arrive like bullets, stay bullet-like for about a week and then before you know it, they're brown. Alternatively, you get a lovely ripe avocado from the greengrocers and within a day it has started to go a little squidgy.

Either way it is always useful to have a few recipes up your sleeve for avocados that aren't 'quite right' and guacamole is one of the best.

Contrary to popular belief, you can freeze guacamole. The trick is to get rid of all the air – contact with air is what turns the guacamole brown. Put the guacamole into a sandwich-size zip-locking freezer bag and push the guacamole into the bottom of the bag. Squeeze the air out of the bag and then seal and freeze. The more lemon or lime in the guacamole, the better it will freeze. To thaw, simply leave in the fridge overnight, or place in a bowl of cool water for about half an hour.

In the same way, if you are storing half an avocado in the fridge, cover the open end with lemon juice and put the avocado inside a sandwich bag. Squeeze as much air out as possible and seal.

If using frozen guacamole I suggest you add the tomatoes fresh, after it has thawed, as frozen and thawed tomatoes tend to be very mushy.

Ingredients

- 2 avocados, preferably over-ripe
- 3 mild chillies, de-seeded and finely chopped
- 1 red onion, finely chopped
- 2 cloves garlic, finely chopped
- 2 tomatoes, de-seeded and finely chopped
- Juice from ½ lemon or lime
- About 4 sprigs fresh coriander
- Pinch of salt to taste
- Tablespoon water (optional)

Leftovers used

Avocados.

Method

1. Spoon out the flesh of the avocado. For under-ripe avocados, use a sharp knife to cut the flesh into quarters and then peel back the skin to remove it.
2. Put the chillies, onion, garlic, tomatoes and coriander into a blender and process until they form a paste.
3. Add the avocado and continue to process until it is thoroughly mixed in. With under-ripe avocados, the guacamole will not be as smooth but don't worry.
4. Add salt to taste.
5. If the mixture is rather solid, add a little water and mix well until it is like a thick paste.
6. Chill and serve with taco chips or pitta bread.

Ham Loaf with Pineapple ⏱ 15 ⏱ 65

This is a particularly good recipe for after Christmas when you might have run out of ideas for how to use up the remains of the ham. You've done the ham sandwiches, the risotto and the cold ham and baked potatoes and still there seems to be copious amounts left...have a go at this, it might just come to the rescue.

There is no reason why you cannot add a few leftover vegetables such as peas, finely chopped carrots or leeks as these will also add some colour to the loaf. However, be careful not to over do these or the loaf might lose its shape when you turn it out.

You will need a large loaf tin for this recipe. This will serve 6-8 people so adjust the quantities according to how much ham you have leftover or how many people you are feeding.

Leftovers used

Breadcrumbs; cooked ham; cooked carrots, leeks, peas.

Method

❶ Preheat the oven to 180°C/350°F/gas mark 4.
❷ Combine all the ingredients for the loaf so they are well mixed in – you may want to use a food processor, using the blending blade.
❸ Using your hands, mould the mixture into a loaf shape and place in a large loaf tin. Using a knife, score the top a few times.
❹ Bake for 30 minutes. Take out of the oven and don't turn the oven off.
❺ Meanwhile, put the ingredients for the glaze, except the pineapple, in a saucepan, bring to the boil and then simmer for 5 minutes allowing the sauce to reduce.
❻ Arrange the pineapple chunks over the loaf and then pour the glaze over the top.
❼ Return to the oven for another 30 minutes, being sure to baste regularly.
❽ Serve immediately with potatoes and seasonal vegetables.

Ingredients

For the loaf:
- 700g of minced or finely chopped ham
- 100g breadcrumbs or rolled oats
- 1 teaspoon dry mustard powder
- Pinch of ground cloves
- 2 eggs, beaten
- 250ml milk

Plus any leftover cooked or raw vegetables, chopped

For the glaze:
- 50ml vinegar
- 75g brown sugar
- 3 tablespoons water
- 1 small tin pineapple chunks

Ingredients

- 10-12 fresh or dried red chilli peppers
- 3 cloves garlic, crushed
- ½ teaspoon salt
- 2 tablespoons olive oil
- 1 teaspoon ground coriander
- 1 teaspoon ground caraway seeds
- ½ teaspoon cumin

Harissa Sauce

 5-30

Harissa is a North African hot pepper sauce which is used extensively with **fish**, **meat**, **couscous** and **soups** to make very spicy dishes which are totally delicious if you like food that bites! The beauty of making your own harissa is that it will keep in the fridge for about 3 months.

This recipe uses fresh or dried chillies, and if you like really spicy harissa then use Cayenne or Chile de Arbol. If, however, you prefer something a little milder, then use New Mexico or Guajillo chillies.

Leftovers used

Fresh or dried chillies.

Method

1. If you're using dried chillies, soak them in water for about half an hour, then remove the stems and seeds.
2. In a food processor blend the chillies, garlic, salt and olive oil until you have a smooth paste.
3. Add the remaining spices and continue to blend.
4. Store in the fridge in an airtight container. From time to time top it up with a little olive oil to stop it drying out.

Harissa with Prawns and Couscous

⏱ 10 ⏱ 10

This recipe for harissa with **prawns** and **couscous** is delicious and a great way of using up any leftover raw or cooked prawns.

Leftovers used

Cooked or raw prawns.

Method

1. Put couscous in a bowl and pour the boiling stock over it, then mix it in with a fork and leave to swell for 5 minutes.
2. Meanwhile, fry the chopped onion and garlic for 2 minutes until soft, add the cumin and continue cooking for another minute.
3. Add the tinned tomatoes and harissa and mix in well. Cook for a few minutes to allow the sauce to thicken slightly.
4. Add the raw prawns and cook for a further 3-4 minutes until they are cooked.
5. For cooked prawns, add them at the last minute and heat through in the sauce.
6. Serve on a bed of couscous with a coriander garnish.

Ingredients for 2 people

- 100g couscous
- 200ml stock
- 1 small onion
- 2 cloves garlic
- 1 teaspoon ground cumin
- 400g tin of tomatoes
- 2-3 teaspoons harissa sauce
- 150g raw or cooked peeled prawns
- Fresh coriander to garnish

Ingredients

- 2 tablespoons vegetable or olive oil
- 1 large onion, chopped
- 1 heaped teaspoon cumin
- 1 teaspoon ground coriander
- 400g tin chick peas (or cannelloni or haricot beans)
- 400g tin chopped tomatoes
- Remains of a jar of pasta sauce (optional)
- Sprig fresh coriander (optional)
- Warm Bread or rolls or chunks of ciabatta

Instant Onion and Bean Stew

 5 ⏰ 10

This is not so much a 'leftovers' recipe as one that can be rustled up in an instant from the store cupboard (a good chance to check that you are well stocked up with the essentials). It is great for those days when there appears to be nothing left in the fridge.

One of the reasons we waste money on unnecessary food and therefore end up throwing it away is that we have lost the ability to 'make something from nothing'. We have become used to looking in the fridge and putting 'Meat' with 'Vegetable' and 'Potato' at best, or putting a 'Ready Meal' straight into the microwave or oven, at worst.

This recipe shows that if you have some basic ingredients you can make a perfectly good and nutritious meal without rushing out the shops and buying more food. Tins of pulses are essential for the store cupboard, they are relatively cheap and keep for months.

Leftovers used

Onion, remains of the pasta sauce.

Method

1. Heat the oil over a medium heat and then add the onions.
2. Cook for about 3 minutes until golden and soft.
3. Add the cumin and stir it into the onions.
4. Add the tin of chick peas or other beans and the tin of tomatoes.
5. Simmer gently until all the ingredients are heated through.
6. Serve with a sprig of coriander on the top and a warmed, fresh bread roll and butter.

Juices

Like smoothies, juices are fantastic for using up **fruit** or **vegetables** that might be a little passed their best but still retain much of their juice and goodness. Using vegetables in their raw form means that none of the goodness has been lost through cooking.

If you have fruit or vegetables that need using up, juice them and freeze the juice in 'portion' sizes so that they can be brought out of the freezer one at a time when necessary. This is a great way of using the second punnet of buy-one-get-one-free fruit that is beginning to be past its best. If you have slightly bruised or over ripe peaches, just purée them in a blender (removing the skins and pit first), then add some sugar to the purée and freeze in an airtight container.

For all these recipes, put all the ingredients into a liquidiser and mix thoroughly. With fruit such as strawberries, passing the juice through a sieve before serving will remove all the little pips, if required. The addition of an apple to some vegetable juices adds some sweetness to the juice.

Variations

Other fruits that are delicious 'juiced up'
- Blueberries
- Blackcurrants
- Cherries
- Melon
- Peaches

Other vegetables that can be used in a 'general' juice
- Artichoke
- Broccoli
- Cabbage
- Red pepper
- Watercress

Leftovers used

Leftover or slightly over-ripe vegetables and fruit: apples, carrots, celery, cranberries, cucumber, grapefruit, oranges, peaches, pears, lemons, raspberries, strawberries, tomatoes.

Carrot and Apple Juice

 5-10

- 3 large carrots, peeled and roughly chopped
- ½ lemon, peeled
- 1 apple

Place all the ingredients in the liquidiser and process until smooth. As an alternative, try adding some beetroot to this juice.

Posh Tomato Juice

 5-10

- 4 tomatoes, skinned, chopped and de-seeded or a tin of chopped tomatoes
- 1 stalk of celery, roughly chopped
- ½ cucumber, peeled and chopped
- ½ teaspoon of sea salt
- Pepper
- Cayenne pepper

Juice the tomato, celery and cucumber in your liquidiser until smooth. Add the salt, pepper and Cayenne pepper to taste.

Spinach and Apple Juice

 5-10

- A bunch of fresh spinach leaves
- 2 apples, peeled, de-seeded and chopped
- ½ lemon, peeled and de-seeded

Combine all the ingredients and blend in the liquidiser.

Apple, Celery and Ginger

5-10

- 3 apples peeled, de-seeded and chopped
- 4 sticks of celery
- Slice of root ginger (to taste)

Combine all the ingredients, making sure you strain the mixture afterwards to remove any of the tough, straggly bits from the celery.

Fruit Punch

5-10

- 6 strawberries/raspberries, fresh or thawed from frozen
- 1 apple, cored, peeled and sliced
- ½ orange, peeled and segmented (or 50ml orange juice)
- 100ml water

Combine all the ingredients and blend in the liquidiser.

Peach, Pear and Apple Juice

- 1 apple, cored, peeled and sliced
- 2 peaches, peeled and stoned
- 1 pear peeled, cored and sliced

5-10

Combine all the ingredients and blend in the liquidiser.

Lemon and Lime Ginger Ale

 5-10

- 2 handfuls of grapes
- 1 apple, cored, peeled and sliced
- 1cm fresh ginger, peeled and chopped
- Juice of one lime
- Juice of half a lemon
- Sparkling water

Mix all the fruit and juice in a blender.
Pour into a glass and top up with the sparkling water and ice.

Strawberry/Raspberry Zing

 5-10

- 2 handfuls of strawberries/raspberries
- 2 medium apples, peeled, cored and sliced
- Juice of ½ lemon

Combine all the ingredients and blend in the liquidiser.

Cranberry Crush

 5-10

- 1 red grapefruit, peeled and segmented
- 2 medium oranges, peeled and segmented
- 3 handfuls cranberries (or 200ml cranberry juice)

Combine all the ingredients and blend in the liquidiser.

Individual Recipes: savoury

Kedgeree

Kedgeree is a classic leftovers meal using leftover fish and a good stock as its main ingredients. In Scotland it is traditionally eaten for breakfast but it makes a good light lunch or supper. Ideally, kedgeree should be made from smoked fish and is a great way of using up any leftover smoked haddock or mackerel but you can use any type of cooked fish or a mixture of two or three different types. Make sure you have removed any bones from the fish by flaking it with a fork.

It is possible to use leftover cooked rice to make kedgeree although the great taste of the dish comes from the fact that the rice absorbs the flavours from the stock and onion as it cooks.

Leftovers used

Smoked or unsmoked, cooked or raw fish such as mackerel, haddock, cod or trout or white crab meat; cooked rice.

Method

1. Boil the eggs for 10 minutes, remove their shells and slice them.
2. Melt the butter in a high sided frying pan or large saucepan over a medium heat. Add the chopped onion and Cayenne pepper or curry powder and fry for about 3 minutes.
3. If using uncooked rice, stir it in so that it is coated in the butter. Add the stock and bay leaf and bring to the boil.
4. Turn the heat down so that it simmers for about 20 minutes.
5. For cooked rice, use only 150ml of stock and cook the onions and Cayenne pepper or curry powder in the stock for about 5 minutes.
6. Meanwhile, if using raw fish, poach it in the milk for about 5 minutes whilst the rice is cooking.
7. Flake the fish using the back of a fork and remove any little bones and skin.
8. When the rice is cooked, take it off the heat and add the flaked fish, tomato ketchup, egg, salt and pepper and half the parsley. Mix all the ingredients well.
9. Season and serve hot with the chopped chives and parsley sprinkled on the top. Add grated Parmesan if using.

Ingredients

- 350g uncooked rice (or equivalent cooked rice)
- 250g smoked (or unsmoked) cooked or raw fish
- 4 eggs
- 50g butter
- 1 medium onion, chopped finely
- 1 teaspoon Cayenne pepper or curry powder
- 750ml good fish, chicken or vegetable stock (or equivalent made with stock cubes)
- 1 bay leaf
- 300ml milk (if using raw fish)
- 2 teaspoons tomato ketchup
- Salt and pepper
- 1 tablespoon chopped parsley
- 1 tablespoon chopped chives
- Grated Parmesan

Individual Recipes: savoury

Lamb Pitta Pockets

⏱ 10 ⏱ 5

Cold **lamb** is delicious, and is almost tastier than when the lamb was first cooked and served hot. With a joint of lamb, it is advisable only to cut the cold meat off the bone when you want to use it, or alternatively freeze the cut lamb meat straight away. This prevents it from drying out.

This recipe is just as delicious using cold **beef**, **chicken** or **turkey** and any number of other ingredients can be added to the 'pocket', for example, sliced up tomatoes, lettuce or roasted vegetables.

It is a good idea to keep some pitta bread in the freezer as it is incredibly useful for snacks, either filled or sliced up to dip in houmous. If pitta bread starts to get a little stale, wet the outside and put in a hot oven for about 2 minutes. This will refresh the bread nicely.

Leftovers used

Cooked lamb, roasted vegetables.

Method

❶ Heat the pitta bread in a toaster.
❷ Melt the knob of butter in a frying pan and add the chopped onion and slices of raw red pepper. Cook for about 3 minutes until the onion is translucent and the pepper soft. If using up roasted vegetables, add these and heat through.
❸ Slice the pitta bread open along the side from one end to the other and spread the inside of the pitta with sour cream.
❹ Fill the pitta pocket with the diced lamb and spoon in the onion and peppers mixture.
❺ Serve with a green salad.

Ingredients

- A small knob of butter
- 1 chopped red/white onion
- 1 sliced red pepper
- 300g diced cooked lamb
- Sliced tomatoes (optional)
- Lettuce (optional)
- Roasted vegetables (optional)
- 4 pitta breads
- Sour cream to taste

Variations

- Beef
- Chicken
- Turkey
- Roasted vegetables Houmous.
- Leeks and hot goat's cheese

Individual Recipes: savoury

Ingredients

- 500g cooked lamb, finely chopped (or leftover, cooked vegetables, chopped)
- 1 onion, chopped
- 1 clove garlic, crushed
- Vegetable oil for frying
- ½ red chilli, finely chopped
- ½ teaspoon cumin seeds
- A large pinch ground coriander
- A large pinch turmeric
- A 2cm piece of root ginger, finely chopped or grated
- Handful of fresh coriander, finely chopped
- 3 sheets filo pastry, sliced in half lengthways

Variations

- Chicken
- Beef
- Vegetable

Lamb Samosas

 20 15

Typically, this dish is used for both **meat** and **vegetables** and, for our purposes, provides a little home for our leftovers. The secret to a good samosa is to create a really delicious taste with the addition of spices, all of which will ideally be in your store cupboard.

I have chosen lamb here but beef or chicken work just as well. Alternatively, a combination of potatoes, cauliflower, peas, carrots or onions will make a delicious vegetable samosa.

Leftovers used

Cooked lamb; cooked vegetables: carrots, cauliflower, peas, potatoes, onions.

Method

1. Heat the oil in a frying pan and fry the onion and garlic for a couple of minutes. Add the cumin seeds, turmeric, ground coriander, chilli and ginger, and cook for 1 minute to release the flavour.
2. Add the cooked lamb and fresh coriander and stir for a further minute until it is coated in the spices. (For vegetable samosas just replace the lamb with the mixed cooked vegetables.)
3. Lay out the filo pastry on a flat surface. For each samosa, put a spoonful of the lamb mixture on one corner of the strip of filo pastry and fold the pastry over the top. Keep folding the pastry around the lamb from corner to corner until you have made a triangle shaped parcel.
4. Repeat this for the remaining samosas.
5. In a heavy frying pan, heat about 4 tablespoons of vegetable oil until it is really hot. Test it by dropping in a bread crumb – if it sizzles then the oil is hot enough.
6. Carefully lay the samosas in the hot oil and fry for a few minutes on each side until the pastry starts to brown and crisp up. Beware, the oil may spit.
7. Remove from the pan using a slotted spoon and drain really well on kitchen paper.
8. Serve hot or cold as a starter with a dollop of sweet chilli sauce.

Leek and Potato Soup

 20 25

This is a really hearty soup and can be served hot or cold but it is delicious hot, with a chunk of really fresh bread to dip in it and lots of cream.

If your leeks are a bit dry, peel off the dry layers and use the rest; keeping them in the vegetable container in the fridge will help stop them drying out. Leeks are at their cheapest during the late autumn and early winter so soup is a great way of using them up, as well as being tasty and warming. This soup can easily be frozen – if you make a lot of it, freeze portions in airtight containers.

Leftovers used

Raw leeks; raw potatoes or cooked potatoes.

Method

1. In a large saucepan, heat the butter and then add the leeks. Cook for about 2 minutes, stirring all the time, until the leeks have softened.
2. Add the celery and raw potato and cook for a further 2 minutes, again stirring constantly to stop the vegetables sticking to the bottom of the pan.
3. Add the stock and black pepper, bring to the boil and then lower the temperature and simmer for about 20 minutes, with a lid on, until the potatoes are completely cooked.
4. If using cooked potatoes, add them in the last few minutes to warm through.
5. Take off the heat, allow to cool for 10 minutes and then purée the soup in a food processor or blender.
6. Before serving, heat the soup through and stir in the cream.
7. Add a garnish of fresh parsley to each bowl of soup.

Ingredients

- 25g butter
- 3 or 4 leeks (depending on the size), chopped
- 1 stick celery, sliced thinly
- 3 medium-sized potatoes, raw or cooked, roughly chopped and peeled
- Approx 1 litre vegetable or chicken stock or equivalent made with stock cubes
- Black pepper
- Half a small carton of cream
- Fresh parsley to garnish

Individual Recipes: savoury

123

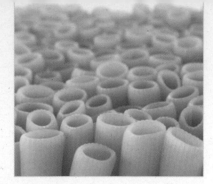

Macaroni Cheese ⏱ 5 ⏱ 10-20

This is a fantastic dish for using up leftovers; it is very easy to cook too much pasta and any left over is often thrown away. However, cold pasta is ideal for macaroni cheese. Don't worry if it is coated in pesto or tomato-based sauce, this enhances the flavour of the macaroni cheese even more. In addition, many other leftovers can be added to make a really filling and quick meal.

Macaroni cheese can be more than just macaroni with a cheese sauce; by using leftovers it can be different every time and much tastier. The variations of meat, poultry and vegetables are endless – anything that can be safely reheated.

For the topping, dip into that bag of frozen breadcrumbs or crunch up any soft crisps and combine the breadcrumbs or crisps with some grated cheese, or slice up tomatoes and lay them on top of the macaroni cheese before sprinkling on the cheese and grilling.

Ingredients

- 100g uncooked pasta per person (or equivalent cooked pasta)
- 70g butter
- 2 tablespoons flour
- 300ml milk
- 70g grated Cheddar cheese
- 1 teaspoon grainy mustard (optional)
- Salt and pepper
- Grated cheese or breadcrumbs for topping

Plus whichever leftover you want to use up.

Variations

- Bacon
- Ham
- Sweet corn
- Roasted vegetables
- Cold sausage
- Chicken

Leftovers used

Cooked pasta; cooked or roasted vegetables; cold, cooked bacon, chicken, ham or sausages.

Method

1. If using uncooked pasta, cook according to the instructions, drain and transfer to a medium-sized ovenproof dish.
2. If using cooked pasta, transfer it straight to the dish.
3. Melt the butter in a saucepan, add the flour and mix well.
4. Gradually blend in the milk, stirring constantly over a medium heat until the sauce becomes thick and smooth.
5. Add the cheese and mustard and cook for a further couple of minutes until the cheese has melted.
6. Add any of your leftover ingredients, mix the sauce well and pour over the pasta.
7. Top with further grated cheese and/or breadcrumbs or stale crisps and place under a hot grill for about 5 minutes or until the topping goes crispy and starts to brown.

Mayonnaise

⏱ 5

It is very rare that eggs become 'leftover' as they are so versatile and can be used in so many different ways, either for a snack or as an ingredient for a main meal. However, there are occasions when we come across recipes that only require part of the egg i.e. just the white, or just the yolk and, like good citizens, we store the remaining unused part in the fridge, to discover it later when it is too late to use it. Mayonnaise is a great way to use up the yolks.

Eggs should really be stored in the fridge although a cool larder or storage area is also fine. Egg shells are porous and therefore unwelcome bacteria can filter through the shell if they are left in a warm place for too long.

Leftovers used

Leftover egg yolks.

Method

❶ Place the egg yolks in a bowl and whisk.
❷ Add the mustard and lemon juice and garlic (if using) and continue to whisk.
❸ Gradually introduce the olive oil, adding a small amount at a time, whisking all the time, until all the olive oil is blended.
❹ Store in the fridge where it should keep for 3-4 days.

Ingredients

(quantities can be adjusted according to how many egg yolks you have left over)
- 2 egg yolks
- 5 tablespoons olive oil
- 1 tablespoon lemon juice
- 1 teaspoon Dijon mustard
- 1 clove garlic (optional)

Mixed Nut and Tofu Roast

⏱ 15 ⏱ 55

In my store cupboard I have a big container which I keep my packets of **nuts** in and every now and again I have a 'spring clean' of the lot and cook this nut loaf. The beauty is that any combination of pine nuts, cashews and walnuts will do so it doesn't matter if you only have a few of one and more of the other.

Tofu has a remarkable ability to absorb the flavours of whatever other ingredients it is cooked with and is therefore extremely versatile. It can be baked, deep fried, shallow fried, marinated, stewed, scrambled, added to soups and casseroles, stuffed into tacos, made into dips . . . the list is endless.

You will need a 25cm x 10cm loaf tin for this.

Leftovers used

Nuts.

Ingredients

- 3 cloves garlic, finely chopped
- 1 onion, peeled and roughly chopped
- 1 teaspoon finely chopped chillies
- 1 pint vegetable stock (or equivalent using stock cubes)
- 25g butter
- 400g tofu, cubed
- About 450g any combination of pine nuts, cashews and walnuts
- 3 eggs
- 110g closed cup mushrooms, finely chopped
- 1 or 2 teaspoons dried basil
- Salt and pepper
- Parmesan

Method

① Preheat the oven to 180°C/350°F/gas mark 4.

② Chop the nuts finely or chop using a food processor.

③ Pour the stock into a large saucepan and add the chopped onion, garlic and chilli. Bring it to the boil and simmer for about 10 minutes.

④ In a bowl, combine the tofu, butter, nuts, eggs, basil and mushrooms. Season with salt and pepper.

⑤ Add the onion and stock to the bowl and stir in well so that the ingredients are well distributed.

⑥ Grease the loaf tin and pour the mixture into the tin. Don't worry if it looks pretty disgusting at this stage!

⑦ Bake it, uncovered, for about 40 minutes until it is set. Test to see if it is cooked by pushing a skewer through it – the skewer should come out clean. If not, put it back in the oven for another 5 minutes.

⑧ Turn loaf out on a plate and sprinkle Parmesan shavings on the top.

⑨ Serve with fresh vegetables.

Pancake Fillings
Savoury and sweet

🕐 10 🕐 15

If you find you are left with pancakes that don't get eaten, pop them in the freezer, with a piece of greaseproof paper between each pancake, and use them another time.

There are numerous combinations of pancake fillings possible, both sweet and savoury. Here are few fillings which are really delicious but you can have fun creating different combinations of your own.

Spinach and Cream Cheese

Ingredients

- 250g spinach (cooked or frozen)
- 1 tablespoon of butter/ margarine
- 1 large onion
- 1 clove garlic, crushed
- A large pinch grated nutmeg
- Black pepper
- 3 tablespoons cream cheese
- Grated Cheddar cheese

Variations

Savoury:

- Chicken and mushroom
- Leek and mushroom in cheese sauce
- Smoked salmon and ricotta cheese

Sweet:

- Bananas and maple syrup
- Bananas with condensed milk
- Sautéed apple with cinnamon and raisins
- Stewed blackberry and apple
- Strawberries, chocolate and whipped cream.

Leftovers used

Cream cheese; cooked pancakes; raw or cooked spinach.

Method

1. Defrost and warm the pancakes in the oven. Cook the spinach, draining it thoroughly through a sieve, pressing it down with a wooden spoon. Set aside.
2. Melt the butter or margarine in a saucepan, add the onion and garlic and cook for about 3 minutes until softened.
3. Stir in the spinach, nutmeg and pepper. Mix well and add the cream cheese. Cook over a low heat for about 3 minutes.
4. Spread the mixture over one side of the pancakes and roll them up.
5. Place the pancakes in an ovenproof dish and scatter grated cheese over them.
6. Cook under a hot grill for about 3-4 minutes until the cheese melts.
7. Serve with a side salad.

Chicken and Mushroom

Leftovers used

Cooked chicken.

Method

1. Preheat the oven to 180°C/350°F/gas mark 4.
2. Melt the butter, over a medium heat, in a saucepan. Add the flour and mix well.
3. Blend in the chicken stock to make a smooth sauce and cook for 20 minutes.
4. Pour half the sauce into a jug and set aside and add the mushrooms to the remaining sauce and bring to the boil. Simmer for 2 minutes.
5. Take off the heat and add the chicken and parsley and mix in well before stirring in the cream.
6. Fill each pancake with the chicken and mushroom sauce and roll them up.
7. Put the pancakes, seam down in an ovenproof dish and pour the remaining sauce over the pancakes, followed by the grated cheese.
8. Bake in the oven for 15 minutes until the cheese has melted.
9. Serve with a green salad.

Ingredients

- 440g cooked diced chicken
- 30g margarine/butter
- 30g flour
- 500ml chicken stock
- 100g sliced mushrooms
- 1 tablespoon chopped parsley
- 100ml cream
- 300g grated hard cheese

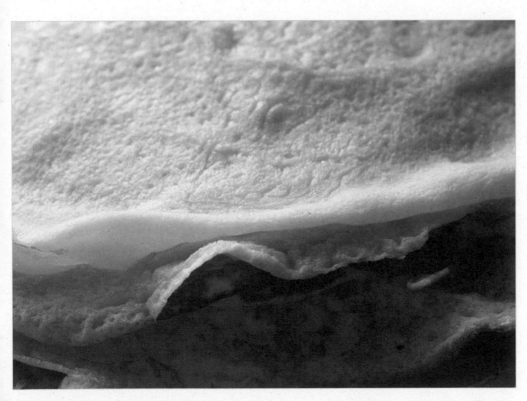

Ingredients

- 6 bananas, thickly sliced
- 200g butter
- 1 dessertspoon soft brown sugar
- 3 tablespoons rum

Variations

- Rum and peach
- Kirsch and pineapple
- Cassis and plum

Rum and Banana

Leftovers used

Soft bananas.

Method

1. Preheat the oven to 180°C/350°F/gas mark 4.
2. In a pan, melt the butter and add the bananas. Cook on a very gentle heat for 20 minutes.
3. When they start to soften, sprinkle over the sugar and half the rum and carry on cooking until the sugar starts to caramelise.
4. When the bananas are cooked, use a slotted spoon to transfer them onto the pancakes. Roll the pancakes up and transfer them to a casserole dish.
5. Pour over the caramelised sauce and the remainder of the rum and bake in the oven for 10 minutes.
6. Serve immediately with a blob of double cream.

Pork Enchiladas

🕐 15 🕐 40

Just about anything can be used as a filling inside tortilla and this is one example which is particularly delicious. However, this recipe works just as well with cooked **chicken** or **beef** so you can experiment. Remember that once cooked meat has been frozen you cannot refreeze it.

This recipe includes making tomato salsa which is extremely easy and quick to make and can be used for so many different recipes as well as providing a delicious dip for raw vegetables or tortilla chips.

The quantities here are for 4 people (2 tortillas each).

Leftovers used

Hard Cheddar cheese; cooked pork; sour cream.

Method

❶ Preheat the oven to 200°C/400°F/gas mark 6.

❷ To make the tortillas:
(a) Combine the flour, baking powder and salt in a bowl and, using your hands, combine the butter until it forms a consistency a bit like breadcrumbs.
(b) Gradually add the water and mix well until the mixture forms a dough. Transfer the dough to a floured surface and divide the mixture into 8.
(c) Roll each piece out until you can cut out a 30cm dough circle (you might want to use a plate as a template).
(d) Heat a non-stick pan on a medium heat and cook each tortilla for 1 minute on each side until it begins to turn golden brown. Remove from the pan and set aside.

❸ To make the salsa: (a) mix all the ingredients together really well in a large bowl.
(b) Remove half the salsa into a separate bowl and mix it with half of the stock.

❹ Add the pork and coriander to the remaining salsa in the bowl and mix well. Season with black pepper.

❺ Warm up the remaining stock and pour into a shallow bowl. Dip the tortillas into the stock until they have softened and have absorbed some of the stock.

❻ Lay out the tortillas and spoon some pork mixture down the centre of each tortilla.

❼ Sprinkle some of the cheese over the tortillas and roll them up. Place the rolled up tortillas, seam down, in a shallow, ovenproof dish.

❽ Pour the salsa and stock mixture over the tortillas, followed by the remainder of the cheese.

❾ Bake in the oven for 30 minutes until the enchiladas are heated right through and bubbling.

❿ Serve with a blob of sour cream on top and garnish with fresh coriander.

Ingredients

- 300-400g cooked pork, cut into slivers
- Handful of fresh coriander leaves, finely chopped
- Black pepper to taste
- 200ml stock, warmed
- 150g Cheddar cheese, grated
- Sour cream

For tomato salsa

- 400g tin chopped tomatoes
- 1 onion, finely chopped
- 1 clove garlic, crushed
- 1 tablespoon tomato purée
- 1 tablespoon mixed herbs
- A glug of olive oil
- Black pepper
- 1 teaspoon curry powder (more if you like it really hot)

For flour tortillas

- 400g plain flour
- ½ teaspoon baking powder
- 75g lard or butter
- Pinch of salt
- 100ml water

Variations

- Beef
- Chicken

Individual Recipes: savoury

Pottage

 10 45

Pottage is a type of rough root **vegetable** soup or stew which dates back to medieval times when food waste was minimal and this was probably on the menu every day in winter when there was a glut of root vegetables! You might not want to eat it every day but it is a great warmer in the cold winter months.

I have given very rough quantities here and basically any combination of **root vegetable** will do, depending on what is available and what you prefer – the greater variety the better. Try, wherever possible, to use vegetables that are in season.

Like all stews and soups that use stock as a main ingredient, the quality of the stock is important. In this recipe you can use **meat**, **chicken** or **vegetable stock** depending on what sort of flavour you want (and what is available).

Pottage can easily be frozen so make lots whilst you have all the ingredients and freeze some for later.

Leftovers used

Raw or cooked potatoes, root vegetables.

Method

1. Dice all the vegetables.
2. Fry the onions in the butter in a large saucepan for about 3 minutes.
3. Add the vegetables and the bay leaves.
4. If the vegetables are raw then cover the pan and cook on a low heat for 10 minutes. Add the stock, cover and simmer for about 20 minutes.
5. If the vegetables are cooked, add the stock and simmer for 5 minutes.
6. Pour half the mixture into a liquidiser and purée. Then add this back into the pan.
7. Stir in the cheese and croutons, season and add a handful of chopped parsley.
8. Serve in nice warm bowls with warm bread rolls.

Ingredients

- 50g butter
- 6 small onions
- 450g cooked or raw potatoes, cut into cubes
- 650g of any combination of raw or cooked carrots, celeriac, parsnips, swede or turnip
- 2 bay leaves
- 1½ pints vegetable stock
- 100g diced cheese (preferably feta but Cheddar will do)
- 2 handfuls croutons

Ratatouille

⏱ 20 ⏱ 15

Although the main ingredient of ratatouille is **aubergine**, which may not be a 'regular' on everybody's shopping list, don't be put off if you don't have an aubergine in the house. There are a number of things that can be added to the basic **peppers** and **tomatoes** version which will make just as delicious a vegetable dish.

Realistically, if you are using up the odd leftover raw vegetable, you will probably only make enough for a side serving of ratatouille, but by increasing the quantities, this can be a delicious vegetarian main dish.

Leftovers used

Raw aubergine, courgettes, peppers, tomatoes.

Method

1. Slice the aubergine and place the slices on a board and sprinkle them with salt. Turn the slices over and repeat. Leave for 5 minutes then wash off with water and drain well on kitchen paper.
2. Score a cross in each tomato and then place them in a pan of boiling water for 1 minute, take out, leave to cool for a few minutes and then peel the skin off. Chop the tomatoes and remove the seeds.
3. Fry the aubergine segments, peppers and courgette in some of the olive oil for about 5 minutes until they are brown all over but not cooked through. Take out and put aside.
4. In the same pan, add the remainder of the oil and fry the onions, garlic and chilli, if using, for about 3 minutes until soft.
5. Stir in the vinegar and sugar and cook for a further minute before adding the tomatoes and half the basil leaves. Mix in well.
6. Add the peppers, aubergine and courgette to the pan and cook for a further 5 minutes.
7. Add any other ingredients and serve garnished with the rest of the basil leaves.

Ingredients

- 3 tablespoons olive oil
- 1 aubergine, sliced
- 2 medium-sized tomatoes, de-skinned and seeded or 400g tin of chopped tomatoes
- 1 red or yellow pepper, diced
- 1 large courgette, sliced
- 1 finely chopped chilli (optional)
- 1 large onion
- 2 cloves garlic
- 1 dessertspoon red wine vinegar
- 1 teaspoon brown sugar
- Handful of fresh basil
- 2 tablespoons salt

Variations

Other ingredients that can be added:

- Roasted pine nuts
- Cubes of feta cheese
- Chopped anchovies
- Grated Parmesan
- Handful of capers

Roasted Vegetable Bruschetta

 15 20

It's very easy to get left with one, or even half, a **courgette** in the vegetable rack and not know what exactly to do with it. Bruschetta is ideal for this situation as just about anything can be popped on top to make a really tasty snack.

Bruschetta itself is a saviour for any baguette that has gone a bit hard – this is especially the case if you are using genuine **French bread** where no preservatives are added to the bread so it goes hard very quickly.

Leftovers used

Stale bread; raw courgettes, peppers, tomatoes, red onions.

Method

❶ Preheat the oven to 220°C/425°F/gas mark 7.
❷ De-seed and slice all the vegetables into thinnish slices and arrange on a baking tray.
❸ In a bowl, mix most of the olive oil and mustard really well and then pour over the vegetables.
❹ With your hands, stir all the vegetables around so that they are coated in the oil and mustard.
❺ Bake in the oven for about 20 minutes until the vegetables brown – you may need to mix them around on the tray a few times to ensure all the vegetables are browned.
❻ Meanwhile, toast the bread slices on both sides. Then rub the garlic over one side of the bread.
❼ When the vegetables are cooked, divide them between the slices and pile them up on the garlicky side of the bread. Drizzle the remaining oil over the slices, scatter with olives and serve with a garnish of fresh basil.

Ingredients

- 300g of any combination of red or yellow peppers, courgette, tomatoes, red onion – sliced
- 3 tablespoons extra virgin olive oil
- 2 teaspoons wholegrain mustard
- 1 baguette or ciabatta loaf, cut into 8 slices
- 1 clove garlic, halved
- 8 pitted olives, thinly sliced (optional)
- Black pepper
- Fresh basil leaves to garnish

Variations

- Mozzarella and tomato
- Goat's cheese and pesto
- Tomato, salami and basil
- Harissa and black olives

Salad Dressings

 5

Lemon Vinaigrette

Just about every part of the **lemon** can be used in cooking, and even when the lemon looks dried up and unattractive the juice is very often still usable; it has hundreds of uses, from pepping up a sauce to preventing discolouration in some fruit and vegetables and the zest is great in cakes and sauces. And of course lemon is a vital ingredient in a good gin and tonic!

Leftovers used

Slightly soft or dried up lemons.

Method

❶ Combine all the ingredients together in a jar and shake really well.

❷ Store in a jar or bottle with a good sealing lid or cork, so that the vinaigrette can be vigorously shaken before each use.

Ingredients

- 5 tablespoons extra-virgin olive oil
- 2 tablespoons freshly squeezed lemon juice
- ½ teaspoon Dijon-style mustard
- ¾ teaspoon fresh thyme leaves, chopped
- 1 clove garlic, crushed
- ¾ teaspoon coarse salt
- Freshly cracked black pepper

Tomato salad dressing

 10

This is delicious either poured over a tomato-based salad or poured into the centre of an **avocado** as the tangy taste makes a pleasant change from normal vinaigrette. If stored in the fridge it will last for several weeks.

Leftovers used

Slightly soft tomatoes.

Method

❶ Put all the ingredients in a food processor or liquidiser and blend until most of the lumps have been removed.

❷ Transfer to a bottle, jar or salad dressing dispenser and chill in the fridge.

Ingredients

· 3 medium tomatoes, de-seeded and chopped
· 2 spring onions, chopped
· 150ml olive oil
· 2 tablespoons red wine vinegar
· 1 tablespoon lemon juice
· Salt and pepper
· 1 teaspoon dried basil
· ½ teaspoon sugar (or more to taste)

Blue cheese dressing

 5

Stilton, and other blue cheeses such as Roquefort and Gorgonzola will freeze well but tend to be rather crumbly when they defrost, which is ideal for this recipe. (If you have bits of leftover blue cheese, freezing them will prevent them drying out.)

Blue cheese dressing is quite rich so use it sparingly. It will not keep for more than about 10 days in the fridge.

Leftovers used

Hard blue cheese.

Method:

❶ Combine all the ingredients in a bowl and mix them well.
❷ Put into a jar and chill in the fridge. Shake really well before serving.

Ingredients

- 150g blue cheese, finely crumbled
- 250ml mayonnaise
- 250ml sour cream
- ¼ onion, grated
- 1 teaspoon mustard powder or English mustard
- Pinch garlic salt (optional)
- 1 teaspoon sugar
- 2 dashes Worcestershire sauce

Spanish Omelette

 10 25

Spanish omelette really is the champion of leftover recipes as it is so versatile, and ideal for using up cooked **vegetables** of all kinds; it is also very quick to prepare.

Spanish omelette or 'tortilla' can be served as a main course or, because it is good served cold, it makes excellent picnic food cut into wedges. In Spain they serve it as tapas, cut into small cubes and speared with cocktail sticks or sandwiched between chunks of **crusty bread**. For a light meal serve with **warm bread** and a **green salad**.

Leftovers used

Cooked vegetables: broad beans, courgettes, French beans, leeks, mushrooms, onions, peas, potatoes, runner beans, tomatoes; cooked bacon, ham, chorizo.

Method

❶ Break the eggs into a bowl and beat them with a fork to mix the white with the yolk. Add the milk and a little salt and pepper to taste. Set this to one side.

❷ Heat the vegetable oil in a deep, non-stick frying pan and fry onions over a medium heat until they are translucent and slightly brown. Add the bacon, ham or chorizo and cook for about 3 minutes.

❸ Chop the cooked potatoes into chunks and add these to the frying pan stirring all the time. Add the rest of your leftover vegetables and heat through.

❹ Add the egg mixture to the pan and add the grated cheese on top.

❺ Lower the heat and cook the omelette for about 15 minutes, occasionally drawing the edge inwards with a palette knife to form a good rounded edge. When there is virtually no runny egg on the top, turn over to cook the other side or put under the grill for a couple of minutes.

❻ Remove from the pan and use a knife to cut the omelette into wedges and serve immediately with a slice of fresh bread and a green salad.

Ingredients

- 1 tablespoon vegetable oil
- 1 red or white onion
- Any streaky bacon/leftover ham/chorizo – chopped
- 3 medium-sized cooked potatoes, diced
- 200g cooked vegetables (peas, French beans, leeks)
- 3-4 eggs
- 3 tablespoons of milk
- 100g grated Cheddar cheese
- Salt and black pepper

Ingredients

- 700g of spiced or smoked sausage, chopped
- 8 tablespoons corn oil
- 150g plain flour
- 2 medium onions, chopped
- 1 green pepper, chopped
- 2 sticks of celery, chopped
- 2 garlic cloves, finely chopped
- 2 pints stock (chicken, beef or vegetable)
- Cayenne pepper
- Tabasco sauce (optional)

Spicy Sausage Stew

 15 60

This is a recipe specifically for spicy or smoked sausage and can either be served in a big bowl with a thick slice of fresh bread or with rice – another great way of using up cooked rice.

Spicy or smoked sausage will store in the fridge for around 2 weeks if kept wrapped up. Spicy sausage such as chorizo is fabulous in a stew, as the fats from the sausage hold a great deal of flavour which is absorbed by the other ingredients.

If you have time, make this stew the day before you want to eat it as, much like a curry, the flavour improves when it is reheated. When reheating, ensure that you transfer the stew from the fridge directly to a heated oven or hob, and reheat thoroughly.

Leftovers used

Cooked spicy or smoked sausage; cooked rice.

Method

❶ Preheat the oven to 160°C/320°F/gas mark 3.

❷ Chop all the vegetables and put to one side.

❸ In a casserole dish, heat the oil until it is really hot. If you are using chorizo, then add the slices to the hot oil and fry for about 2 minutes.

❹ Add the flour and mix in thoroughly until the mixture turns brown.

❺ Add the vegetables and sauté them over a medium heat until they soften.

❻ Add the stock a bit at a time, stirring well after adding each amount, to make a smooth sauce.

❼ Add the remaining cooked spicy or smoked sausage and season with Cayenne pepper (and a few drops of Tabasco if you want it extra spicy).

❽ Cook in the oven for about 1 hour.

❾ Serve with rice or chunks of fresh bread. If you are reheating cooked rice, then make sure it is heated up quickly and thoroughly.

Stuffed Peppers with Rice

⏱ 15 ⏱ 35

Cooked rice must never remain at room temperature for any length of time, either when it has just been cooked, or when it has been taken from the fridge to be added to a dish.

Therefore, once rice is first cooked, allow it to cool and then transfer it straight to the fridge or freezer. Likewise, when you are cooking with cooked rice, take the rice straight from the fridge to a hot oven or wok, frying pan etc. When using frozen rice, a top tip is to smack the bag on the side of the kitchen counter before thawing – this loosens up the rice grains.

This dish can be served as a delicious starter or light lunch on its own or is equally good accompanying meat such as chicken or lamb.

Leftovers used

Cooked, chopped bacon bits; cooked ham; cooked broccoli, mushrooms, onions, peas, spinach; cheese.

Method

❶ Preheat the oven to 190°C/375°F/gas mark 5.

❷ Cut the tops off the peppers (making about a 4cm diameter circle around the stalk) and spoon or cut out all the white bits and seeds inside. Keep the 'lids' of the peppers.

❸ Drain the juice from the tinned tomatoes or, if using fresh tomatoes, separate the flesh of the tomato from the juice and seeds as much as possible.

❹ Fry the chopped onion in the oil over a medium heat for 2 minutes. Add the garlic and fry for a further minute.

❺ In a bowl, mix the tomatoes, cooked rice, oregano, parsley, onions, garlic and any of the leftovers you want to add (finely chopped). Season well.

❻ Put the peppers, open end up, on a deep baking tray. Spoon the rice mixture into the peppers so that they have equal amounts in each. Replace the lids on the peppers.

❼ Put a little water (about half an inch) in the baking tray – this will prevent the peppers from burning – and put them in the oven for 30 minutes until the peppers are cooked.

❽ Serve hot on its own or with chicken or lamb.

Ingredients

- 8 peppers, yellow or red
- 2 onions, finely chopped
- 1 tablespoon oil
- 2 large cloves garlic
- 400g tin chopped tomatoes or 6 large tomatoes, chopped
- 400g cooked rice (100g per person)
- 4 sprigs fresh parsley/3 teaspoons dried parsley
- 2 teaspoons dried oregano
- Salt and pepper to taste

Plus any leftovers you want to add (finely chopped).

Variations

- Nuts
- Seeds

Individual Recipes: savoury

Sweet Potato and Prawn Cakes

⏱ 15 ⏱ 15

Sweet potatoes are often a forgotten vegetable and yet they are relatively cheap and very versatile. I think they are best when they are baked in the oven in their skins, like a baked potato, and served with a dollop of butter in the middle.

This recipe is ideal if you should find you have either a lonely sweet potato in your vegetable rack or have some cooked sweet potato left in the fridge. It is also a delicious way to use up leftover cooked prawns, which only last in the fridge for 2-3 days.

Leftovers used

Cooked prawns; raw or cooked sweet potato.

Ingredients

- 500g sweet potato
- 6 tablespoons groundnut or sunflower oil
- 1 onion finely, chopped
- 1 red & 1 green chilli, halved de-seeded and finely chopped
- 4 cloves garlic, finely chopped
- 2 teaspoons ground cumin
- 250g cooked prawns (cut into chunks if big)
- A little oil for frying
- Handful of fresh coriander, finely chopped
- 3 tablespoons plain flour

Method

❶ If you are using raw sweet potato, bake in a pre-heated oven at 190°C/375°F/gas mark 5 until tender – how long depends on the size of the potatoes but timings will be similar to normal baked potatoes. Leave until cool enough to handle then remove and discard the skin.

❷ Heat 2 tablespoons of the oil in a frying pan and sauté the onion and chilli until soft but not coloured. Add the garlic and cumin and cook for 2 more minutes to release the fragrance.

❸ Mash the onion mixture together with the sweet potato flesh and plenty of salt and pepper.

❹ Add the prawns, coriander and flour and mix well. Season with salt and pepper and then put in the fridge to firm up a little.

❺ With floured hands, form the mixture into little balls and pat down, lightly coat each one in flour. If you are making the cakes in advance (which is a good idea) put them in an airtight container and refrigerate.

❻ To cook them, heat the oil in a frying pan and fry the cakes in batches until golden on both sides and hot through – four or five minutes each side. Treat them gently as they are fragile.

❼ Delicious served with a tamarind sauce and a cucumber raita.

Tomato and Fennel Gazpacho

🕐 10 🕐 50

Fennel is a vegetable that is often bought in a fit of enthusiasm, only to sit in the vegetable rack for an age while you think of something to do with it.

Here is a great gazpacho recipe that uses that bulb of fennel left in the vegetable rack and also finds a home for any slightly overripe **tomatoes** you may have.

Leftovers used

Croutons; fennel; soft or leftover tomatoes.

Method

1. Skin the tomatoes by scoring a cross on the skin of each tomato and placing them in boiling water for a minute. Remove the tomatoes from the water, allow to cool slightly and the skins should come away easily.
2. Trim the green fronds from the fennel (but keep them for garnish) and cut the bulb into quarters. Cut out the central stem and slice into thinnish slices. Put in a saucepan with a little salt and water. Bring to the boil, put the lid on and simmer for 10 minutes. Keep the water for later.
3. Crush the coriander seeds and peppercorns in a pestle and mortar.
4. Heat the olive oil and add the crushed seeds and peppercorns along with the chopped onion. Cook for about 2 minutes, then add the garlic and cook for a further 2 minutes.
5. Add balsamic vinegar, lemon juice, chopped tomatoes and oregano. Stir well.
6. Add the fennel and its cooking water.
7. Stir in the tomato purée, bring everything to simmering point and simmer gently (without a lid) for 30 minutes.
8. When it has cooled sufficiently, transfer to a liquidiser or food processor and process just enough for there to be a few lumps left in.
9. Chill in the fridge for several hours and serve really cold with croutons and garnish with the chopped up fennel fronds. You may want to add a few ice cubes to it at the last minute.

Ingredients

- 4-5 medium-sized tomatoes
- 1 medium onion, chopped
- 1 large fennel bulb
- 1-2 cloves garlic, crushed
- 1 teaspoon coriander seeds
- ½ teaspoon peppercorns
- 1 tablespoon balsamic vinegar
- 1 tablespoon lemon juice
- 1 tablespoon extra virgin olive oil
- ¾ teaspoon chopped fresh oregano
- 1 small squeeze tomato purée
- 1 rounded teaspoon salt (preferably rock salt)

Individual Recipes: savoury

Tsatsiki

 15

Tsatsiki is a tangy Greek **yoghurt** sauce which can also double as an appetizer or dip. It is the classic accompaniment for souvlaki, a classic Greek dish made from marinated pork or lamb, and it can also be served with Indian and Middle Eastern food, shish kebabs and spicy curry.

Tsatsiki is a great summer dish, served with a selection of fresh crudités or taco chips it makes a fine accompaniment to a glass of cold, crisp white wine. It is best with sweet tasting **cucumbers,** which are in abundance in the summer, and it is also a fine way of using up the end of a cucumber.

Tsatsiki is not suitable for freezing, as cucumbers will go soggy if they are frozen, but it will store in the fridge for several days if covered. In fact, the sauce actually improves with overnight storage, since this allows the flavours to mix more evenly.

Tsatsiki is also delicious served with spicy fish cakes or prawn cakes with sweet chilli sauce.

Leftovers used

Half a cucumber.

Method

1. Crush the garlic cloves in a pestle and mortar so that you retain all the juice from the garlic.
2. Peel and de-seed the cucumber and then chop it very finely (or grate it) and place the chopped cucumber on a piece of kitchen roll to drain the water.
3. Mix the cucumber with the garlic in a bowl and add the olive oil and red wine vinegar.
4. Add the yoghurt to the cucumber mixture. Mix really well so that the ingredients are all combined.
5. Chill for 24 hours to allow the garlic flavours to infiltrate the yoghurt.
6. Serve with raw chopped vegetables or taco chips and garnish with mint.

Ingredients

- 470ml Greek or natural yoghurt
- 2 cloves of garlic (or more according to taste)
- ½ medium cucumber
- Juice from half a lemon
- 1 tablespoon extra virgin olive oil
- Pinch of salt
- Mint to garnish

Turkey and Broccoli Hollandaise

🕐 25 🕐 40

This recipe is great for after using up both **turkey** meat and stuffing after Christmas and is a delicious meal in its own right. Obviously, the taste will vary according to what stuffing you have cooked with the turkey – this can range enormously from the classic sage and onion to something like apricot and walnut.

If you don't want to make stuffing, a packet of stuffing mix will work just as well. You can use leftover **egg** yolks to make the hollandaise sauce; making your own sauce is cheaper and nicer than a bought jar, is very easy and takes no time at all.

Leftovers used

Cooked turkey and stuffing.

Method

❶ Preheat the oven to 160°/325°F/gas mark 3.
❷ To make the sauce: blend the egg yolks in a food processor or blender with some black pepper for about 1 minute.
❸ Heat the lemon juice and white wine vinegar in a saucepan until it starts to simmer. Then gradually add the mixture to the egg yolks, blending as you add each bit.
❹ Melt the butter in the saucepan and very gradually blend in the butter into the egg mixture.
❺ For the rest of the dish: steam the broccoli florets for about 5 minutes and then drain.
❻ Meanwhile, fry the onions in a little butter for about 3-4 minutes until they are soft.
❼ In an ovenproof dish, make a layer of stuffing on the bottom of the dish, followed by a layer of the turkey meat and broccoli. Season with salt and pepper.
❽ Pour over the hollandaise sauce and bake in the oven for 25-30 minutes until it has heated through.
❾ It is delicious served with a baked potato and some crunchy carrots.

Ingredients

For the hollandaise sauce
- 2 large egg yolks
- 1 dessertspoon lemon juice
- 1 dessertspoon white wine vinegar
- 110g butter
- Salt and pepper

For the turkey dish
- 100g broccoli florets
- 350g stuffing (or a packet of stuffing mix)
- 250g cooked turkey
- 1 red onion, sliced
- Knob of butter

Vegetable and Lentil Bake

 10 ⏱ 60

This is a very easy recipe for using up any spare **vegetables** and really any combination will do. Although this is essentially a vegetable bake, if you have a few slices of **salami**, **chorizo** or **ham**, add these to the bake together with any hard ends of **cheese** – Parmesan, Cheddar, Gruyère etc. will also find a home here.

Lentils will keep for a long time in the store cupboard and are cheap and easy to cook, so are an ideal staple for the kitchen. The beauty of them is that they absorb and hold flavour – a really good **stock** will provide a really good tasting lentil bake.

Leftovers used

Raw butternut squash, raw or cooked broccoli, carrots, leeks, sweet potato, swede, turnip; raw or cooked peas; cooked ham or gammon; salami or chorizo.

Method

❶ Preheat the oven to 200°C.

❷ Heat the oil over a medium heat in a large frying pan, add the onions and garlic, cook for about 3 minutes, until onions are soft.

❸ Add chorizo or salami if using and fry for another 2 minutes.

❹ Add the uncooked vegetables and cook for a further 2 minutes, stirring occasionally to coat the vegetables in oil.

❺ Add the uncooked lentils, cook for a further 2 minutes.

❻ Stir in the water and reduce the heat a little and simmer until most of the water has been absorbed. Stir in the lemon juice.

❼ Add half the vegetable stock and simmer until it has been absorbed. Keep adding more stock, as needed, until the vegetables are cooked and the lentils are soft and mushy and no longer absorbing the stock. This takes approximately 25-30 minutes.

❽ Add half the cheese, any cooked vegetables or cooked ham or gammon and mixed herbs, and mix in well.

❾ Transfer to an ovenproof dish and sprinkle the top with the remaining cheese and pine nuts or sesame seeds.

❿ Bake in the oven for 20 minutes until cheese bubbles and turns light brown. Serve on its own or delicious as an accompaniment to sausages, a meat stew or casserole.

Ingredients

- A good slug of vegetable or olive oil
- 1 large onion, finely chopped
- 1 large garlic clove, finely chopped
- Sliced or cubed ham, chorizo, salami (optional)
- 250g combination of raw or cooked vegetables (as above)
- 200g uncooked red lentils
- Juice of one lemon
- 250ml water
- 500ml vegetable stock (fresh, stock cubes or Bouillon powder)
- 1 teaspoon mixed herbs
- 120g grated Cheddar
- Handful of pine nuts or sesame seeds

Roasted Vegetable and Halloumi Kebabs
with spaghetti

⏱ 10 ⏱ 15

Kebabs look fantastic on a barbecue in summer as the colours make such a lovely contrast and jazz up the food. This recipe is ideal for when you have a few, lonely raw **vegetables** left over and the beauty is that you don't need very much of any one thing. Use summer vegetables such as **courgettes, onions** and **peppers** when they are at their least expensive.

You can also use up any leftover cooked **spaghetti**, which is delicious quickly reheated and tossed in basil and olive oil.

Leftovers used

Raw summer vegetables: courgettes, mushrooms, onions, peppers; cooked spaghetti.

Method

❶ Light the barbecue (or turn on the grill so it is nice and hot).

❷ Finely chop the basil and mix in a bowl with the olive oil and black pepper.

❸ Add the chopped vegetables and halloumi to the bowl and stir it so it is coated in the basil and oil.

❹ If you're using uncooked spaghetti, cook it according to the instructions, drain and put to one side.

❺ Thread the vegetables and halloumi onto skewers ensuring that there is a good variety on each skewer.

❻ Cook on the barbecue (or under the grill) for 10-15 minutes, turning half way through so the kebabs cook on both sides.

❼ If using cooked spaghetti, boil a kettle and pour the boiling water over it, using a fork to tease the spaghetti to stop it sticking together. If it is still a bit sticky, add in a little olive oil.

❽ Pour the remains of the basil and oil mixture into a saucepan and warm gently. Add the spaghetti and toss for a minute until the spaghetti is covered in the basil and oil.

❾ Add roasted pine nuts to the spaghetti and serve with the kebabs.

To roast pine nuts: Dry fry them over a high heat, for 5 minutes, stirring continually to stop them burning.

Ingredients

- 50g fresh basil
- 5-6 tablespoons olive oil
- Cracked black pepper
- 250g halloumi, drained and cubed
- 1 large red pepper, cut into cubes and de-seeded
- 8 large mushrooms, halved
- 1 medium courgette, cut into 2cm thick slices
- 3 red onions, quartered
- 2 tablespoons pine nuts, roasted
- 400g cooked/uncooked spaghetti

Vegetable Stew

 **15** **20-40**

Vegetable stew is the best way to use up any lonely, maybe slightly wrinkly vegetables and it doesn't matter if you only have one of everything.

Just about any combination will do but it is obviously cheaper and better for the environment to use vegetables in season, rather than those which have been flown in, so I have made a suggestion for both winter and summer stews using 'in season' vegetables.
Vegetable stew is delicious served with warm chunks of fresh bread.

Leftovers used

Winter stew: Raw butternut squash, carrot, celery, lentils, parsnips, potato, swede, sweet potato, turnip.
Summer stew: Raw broad beans, carrot, courgette, green beans, mushrooms, red peppers, tomatoes.

Method

1. Wash, peel, core and chop all the vegetables into bite-sized chunks.
2. Heat the oil and cook the onions for 2 minutes. Add the garlic, and any spices or chilli (if using), and cook for a further minute.
3. Add the remaining vegetables and cook for about 3 minutes, stirring all the time.
4. Add the stock, tomato purée and Worcestershire sauce, if using, and season with salt and pepper.
5. Bring to the boil, then reduce the heat. For summer vegetables, simmer for about 15 minutes, for winter vegetables, 35-40 minutes until the vegetables are cooked.
6. Serve with a thick slice of fresh bread.

Ingredients

- 900g combination of vegetables (see right)
- 3 tablespoons oil
- 2 onions
- 2 cloves garlic
- 400g tinned chopped tomatoes
- 500ml vegetable stock
- 1 tablespoon tomato purée
- A dash of Worcestershire sauce (optional)
- 2 celery sticks, salt and pepper

Optional Ingredients

- 1 teaspoon ground cumin
- 1 teaspoon ground coriander
- 1 teaspoon chilli powder
- 1-2 teaspoons Worcestershire sauce

Individual Recipes: sweet

Apple and Cinnamon Fritters

 20 10

Let's face it, no-one likes eating wrinkly **apples**, and they are often left in the fruit bowl. This is a great recipe for using them up and making a delicious pudding.

This recipe also works well with **pears** and can come to the rescue if you happen to buy some pears that are not as juicy and flavoursome as they could be. Don't throw them away, make fritters – the cinnamon gives a lovely spicy taste which disguises any blandness from the fruit itself.

Leftovers used

Wrinkly apples or pears.

Method

1. Heat the oil in a saucepan.
2. Peel the apples, core them using a corer or sharp knife and slice into rings.
3. Place the flour, corn flour, sugar and salt into a large bowl. Gradually beat in the egg and enough milk to form a batter (about ¼ pint milk).
4. Dip the apple rings into the batter and coat well.
5. Fry the fritters until golden (about 3-4 minutes).
6. Remove the fritters from the oil with a slotted spoon and drain on absorbent kitchen paper.
7. Sprinkle generously with sugar and cinnamon.
8. Serve drizzled with cream and honey.

Ingredients

- 3 tablespoons vegetable oil
- 2 apples
- 110g plain flour
- 1 teaspoon corn flour
- Pinch of caster sugar
- Salt
- 1 egg
- ¼ pint (150ml) milk

To serve:

- Sprinkle of caster sugar
- Sprinkle of cinnamon
- Double cream to drizzle (or natural yoghurt)
- Honey to drizzle (optional)

Variations

- Pear fritters

Baked Apples and Pears ⏱ 10 ⏱ 25-30

Pears can quite quickly develop soft, brown areas on them as they go from being ripe to being slightly over ripe. However, there is no reason why the brown bits cannot be cut out and the rest of the pear eaten raw or, sometimes even better, baked. Here is a suggestion for just such an occasion.

For this recipe, try to use an **apple** that is quite tart – Bramleys are great and grown in the UK. Granny Smiths are also good but, contrary to popular belief, these are not grown in the UK. Rocha and Comice pears are my favourite for this pudding as they have a slightly creamy textured flesh and are very juicy.

The best way to serve this is with **crème fraîche** or **ice cream** or you could be really naughty and serve with a blob of clotted cream, which tastes absolutely delicious with the sugar and brandy or Calvados.

Leftovers used

Wrinkly apples or pears.

Method

❶ Preheat the oven to 180°C/350°C/gas mark 4.
❷ Arrange the prepared apples and pears in an oven proof dish and put the cinnamon stick in amongst the fruit.
❸ In a small bowl, mix the butter, sugar and nutmeg together and then arrange the mixture around the fruit.
❹ Add a little bit of water and brandy or Calvados, if you have any, to stop the fruit from sticking to the bottom of the dish.
❺ Bake in the oven for about 25-30 minutes, basting occasionally to keep the fruit moist.
❻ Serve with a dollop of crème fraîche, ice cream or clotted cream.

Ingredients

· 2 or 3 soft pears, peeled, cored and quartered
· 2 or 3 apples, peeled, cored and cut into eighths
· 2 sticks of cinnamon
· 1 teaspoon nutmeg
· 2 tablespoons soft brown or Muscovado sugar
· 1 tablespoon brandy or Calvados (optional)
· 2 tablespoons butter
· Water

Variations

· Baked peaches and pears
· Brandy
· Red wine

Individual Recipes: sweet

Banana and Chocolate Digestive Pudding

 10-60

This was my favourite pudding when I was a child and consequently has been a regular feature on our table at the weekends. The beauty of it is that it takes about 5 minutes to prepare and combines the sweetness of the bananas with the crunch of the chocolate biscuit. Definitely one for those with a sweet tooth!

Not only is it a perfect way to use up any bananas that are getting rather soft, but it also finds a home for any slightly soft chocolate digestive biscuits or the remains of biscuits at the bottom of the biscuit tin.

Recently I tried this recipe using ginger biscuits and it was fantastic – although it got the thumbs down from the children as it had no chocolate in it! So chocolate covered ginger biscuits might be a good compromise!

Leftovers used

Over-ripe bananas and stale biscuits.

Method

❶ Mash up the bananas in a flat-bottomed dish.
❷ Add the yoghurt, brown sugar and lemon juice and mix well.
❸ Tear off two sheets of kitchen roll (still attached to each other) and lay out flat.
❹ Roughly break the biscuits onto one sheet of the kitchen roll and fold the second sheet over the top of the biscuits.
❺ Crush the biscuits inside the kitchen roll with a rolling pin, making sure you crush all the lumps.
❻ Sprinkle crushed biscuits on top of the banana mix and flatten down with a fork.
❼ Put the pudding in the fridge for an hour before serving.

Ingredients

- 3 or 4 ripe bananas (depending on the size)
- 250g natural yoghurt (or double cream)
- 2 tablespoons brown sugar
- squeeze of lemon juice (optional)
- 6 or 7 chocolate digestive biscuits (or any other leftover biscuits or crumbs in the bottom of the biscuit tin)

Banana and Yoghurt Scotch Pancakes

⏱ 10 ⏱ 15

There are so many fantastic recipes for brown bananas which are cheap to buy – you can save money and have delicious puddings at the same time, as well as using something you might otherwise throw away as unusable.

Happily the ridiculous EU regulation which stated that bananas must be "free of abnormal curvature" and at least 14 cm in length was overturned recently, so the future of the bent banana is safe and they are no longer being left to rot!

This recipe is ideal for using up brown bananas and any natural yoghurt you have in the fridge. The pancakes are delicious either served with just butter or with maple or golden syrup.

Leftovers used

Brown bananas, leftover natural yoghurt.

Method

1. In a food processor, mix up the egg, mushed up bananas, yoghurt and milk.
2. Mix the flour, sugar, salt and baking powder together and add to the mixture, a bit at a time, and mix thoroughly until it forms a batter.
3. Transfer the batter to a jug. Don't worry if there are a few lumps of banana.
4. Heat a knob of butter and a tablespoon of oil in a pan. When hot, turn the heat down a little, spoon the batter into the pan, making little pancakes.
5. Cook on both sides until golden brown.
6. You will need to cook in batches to use up all the batter, keeping the cooked ones warm until you have enough.
7. Serve warm with maple syrup or crème fraîche.

Ingredients

- 2 brown bananas, mashed
- 2 heaped tablespoons natural or Greek yoghurt
- 1 egg
- 125ml milk
- 2 teaspoons baking powder
- 150g plain flour
- 1 tablespoon sugar
- A pinch of salt
- Butter and oil for frying

Individual Recipes: sweet

Banana Bread

 15 ⏲ 60

Soft, brown bananas are ideal for this recipe which is great as they are often ignored if left in the fruit bowl. Bananas release energy slowly over a period of time so banana bread is ideal for a mid-morning school snack or, in my case, any-time-of-the-day naughty moment! Much better than the sugar rush followed by an energy 'low' that is gained from confectionery.

I have included the option to add any spare **nuts** you may have leftover in the store cupboard or even some **chocolate** drops, although the chances of them being around for long are slim!

You will need a 25cm x 10cm loaf tin.

Leftovers used

Slightly soft or over-ripe bananas; slightly off milk; chocolate drops (optional); nuts (optional).

Ingredients

- 3 large or 4 medium ripe/over-ripe bananas
- 180g brown sugar
- 125g butter
- 1 teaspoon vanilla essence
- 2 eggs
- 1 teaspoon ground Cinnamon
- 250g plain flour
- 1 teaspoon bicarbonate of soda
- 3 tablespoons milk, at room temperature
- 150g chocolate drops (optional)
- 75g halved walnuts or pecan nuts (optional)

Method

1. Preheat the oven to 180°C/350°F/gas mark 4.
2. Grease the inside of the loaf tin.
3. Mush the bananas with the back of a fork until they are reasonably smooth.
4. Put the butter and sugar in a food mixer and whisk until creamy. Add bananas, eggs, vanilla, cinnamon and a pinch of salt and whisk until all the ingredients have combined.
5. Add the flour and bicarbonate of soda and whisk again until the mixture is smooth.
6. Finally add the lukewarm milk. Mix in well.
7. Add the chocolate drops/walnuts/pecans to the mixture, give it all a good stir and scrape the mixture into the loaf tin.
8. Cook in the oven for 1 hour. Test to see if it is cooked by putting a skewer down through the centre of the cake – the skewer should come out clean. If not, put back in the oven for another 5 minutes.
9. Turn out onto a cooling tray and leave to cool for about 20 minutes.
10. Store in an airtight container.

Blueberry Muffins

⏱ 10 ⏱ 20

Blueberries are a 'super food', full of fantastic antioxidants so this is a great way to get a dose of goodness. You don't need a huge amount of fruit to make the muffins so they are an extremely good way of using up any that are left over.

This is a variation of the 'basic cake mix' and muffins can be frozen easily so you can make a big batch and freeze half. You can use this recipe with any type of summer fruit, and in different combinations.

Leftovers used

Raw blueberries or any leftover summer fruit.

You will need some paper muffin cases/large fairy cake cases for this recipe.

Method

❶ Preheat the oven to 200°C/400°F/gas mark 6.
❷ Place 6-8 muffin cases on a baking tray, evenly spaced. You will probably need 2 baking trays as this mixture makes about 8-10 muffins.
❸ Cream the butter and sugar in a food processor until it makes a smooth paste.
❹ Mix the eggs in one at a time, until they are all blended in.
❺ Add the flour, baking powder and nutmeg and mix well.
❻ Place a good spoonful of mixture into each muffin case, so that the cases are filled to about half way. Push about 6-8 blueberries into each muffin by hand.
❼ Bake in the oven for 20 minutes or until golden on top.
❽ Cool on a cooler rack and store in an airtight container.
❾ Delicious served with Greek yoghurt, clotted cream or ice cream.

Ingredients

- 110g butter
- 70g caster sugar
- 2 eggs
- 110g plain flour
- 1 heaped teaspoon baking powder
- A pinch of nutmeg
- About 150g fresh or frozen blueberries or other summer fruit

Variations

- Blackcurrant and raspberry
- Strawberry and chocolate

Individual Recipes: sweet

Bread and Butter Pudding

 15 35

This is a delicious, old fashioned winter pudding, very easy to make, which uses up any stale white bread or excess of bread in the bread bin – it mustn't be too fresh and make sure you keep the crusts on.

As with many recipes, you can vary the extras, and if you have any egg yolks left over from making meringues then you can add them as well.

You can freeze bread and butter pudding successfully but make sure you thaw it out slowly and thoroughly. Do not try to refreeze the pudding again, however, as it uses milk which contains bacteria which may become harmful if frozen and thawed more than once.

Personally I like to smother bread and butter pudding in custard when I serve it – if you have any leftover custard, here's your chance to use it.

Ingredients

- 8 slices buttered bread cut in half diagonally
- 40g sultanas or currants
- Rind of lemon or orange (grated)
- 250ml full fat milk
- 70ml double cream
- 50g caster sugar
- 3 eggs
- Nutmeg

Variations

- Lemon/orange peel
- Sultanas/currants
- Nutmeg
- Chocolate chips

Leftovers used

Stale bread.

Method

1. Preheat the oven to 180°C/350°F/gas mark 4.
2. Place one layer of the bread into the base of a well-buttered baking dish and sprinkle over some sultanas.
3. Repeat with another layer of bread and sultanas and carry on with the layers until all the bread and sultanas are used.
4. Beat the egg, milk, cream, peel and sugar together and then pour over the bread.
5. Grate some nutmeg over the top and bake in the oven for 35 minutes. The top should be golden and crisp looking when it's finished.
6. Serve hot with cream or custard.

Caramelised Oranges

🕐 15 🕐 15

This recipe is an excellent way to use up any slightly dried-out oranges that are past their best but still contain a decent amount of juice inside. This is such a quick, simple recipe and I have offered a 'grown-up' version as well as one that you can give the children.

Oranges do last for a relatively long time but try and keep them out of a warm environment as this dries them out more quickly. One way to preserve oranges is to cut them into quarters and freeze them in a plastic bag.

Try this dish with a dollop of Greek yoghurt on the side.

Leftovers used

Slightly soft or wrinkly oranges.

Method

❶ Carefully cut or scrape off the zest (the very outer surface) of half of one of the oranges.
❷ Peel the oranges, making sure you remove all the pith.
❸ Thinly slice the oranges and arrange in a flat-bottomed dish.
❹ For the adult version, pour the Cointreau over the oranges and preferably set them aside for about 1 hour.
❺ Meanwhile put the water, sugar and zest from the orange in a saucepan over a gentle heat and stir until the sugar has dissolved. For the child-friendly version, add the cinnamon stick to the water.
❻ Bring to the boil and let the water simmer until it has reduced by about half and the sugar has caramelised to form a thickish solution.
❼ Take the mixture off the heat and allow to cool.
❽ Pour over the oranges and chill in the fridge.
❾ Serve with a garnish of mint leaves.

Ingredients

- 4 oranges
- Zest from half of one of the oranges
- 2 tablespoons Cointreau, or failing that another brandy-based liqueur (adult version)
- 1 cinnamon stick (child-friendly version)
- 150ml water
- 3 tablespoons sugar
- Fresh mint for decoration

Ingredients

- 225g plain chocolate
- 3 tablespoons golden syrup (or maple syrup)
- 50g margarine
- 100g crisp cereal (e.g. cornflakes)

Chocolate Crispy Cakes 5 10

As well as being a good way to use up slightly soft breakfast cereal, it can be a great way to get any young children learning about basic cooking, having fun and getting very chocolatey at the same time. It is vital that we pass on any cooking skills that we have, so that children develop an enthusiasm for food and a knowledge of how to prepare it. With a basic knowledge and some resourcefulness, we can crack the problem of food waste.

Breakfast cereals can be kept for several weeks if they are stored properly, i.e. with the inner greaseproof lining folded down. Alternatively, use a plastic clip or clothes peg to seal the packet.

You will need to allow about two hours for the chocolate to set in the fridge.

Leftovers used

Any kind of crisp cereal, perhaps past its best e.g. rice crispies or cornflakes.

Method

❶ Grease the inside of a 20cm diameter shallow tin using a little butter. Try not to leave too much butter on the tin.

❷ Break the chocolate into a large pan. Add the syrup and margarine.

❸ Heat the mixture gently, stirring all the time.

❹ When the chocolate has melted, add the cornflakes or rice crispies and stir well so that they are coated all over in the chocolate.

❺ Spoon the mixture into the tin and gently smooth the top with the back of a spoon. Let the mixture cool.

❻ Put the tin in the fridge until the chocolate has set – approximately two hours.

❼ Use a sharp knife to cut it into eight pieces.

Christmas Date Biscuits ⏱ 15 ⏱ 15

Semi-dried **dates** are a luxury and they really only get brought out once a year to decorate the Christmas dinner table. You are often left with at least half a tray of dates which can sit in the store cupboard for months on end while you think of something to do with them.

Well, here is a great idea which is extremely easy to prepare and very tasty. The stickiness of the dates makes the biscuits really chewy and delicious. Once you have made them, store the biscuits in an airtight biscuit tin. Dates are also suitable for freezing.

Leftovers used

Semi-dried dates.

Method

❶ Preheat the oven to 180°C/350°F/gas mark 4.
❷ Lightly grease 2 or 3 baking trays.
❸ Put the flour in a large mixing bowl, add the butter and rub in with your fingertips until the mixture resembles breadcrumbs.
❹ Stir in the sugar, dates and nutmeg and mix well to evenly distribute the ingredients.
❺ Add the egg yolks and mix to a dough.
❻ Turn onto a floured surface and roll out to 5mm/ ¼ inch thickness. Cut into shapes with a biscuit or pastry cutter.
❼ Transfer to the baking trays and bake in the oven for 10-15 minutes until golden brown.
❽ Take out of the oven and cool on cooling racks.
❾ Serve with some vanilla ice cream.

Ingredients

Makes approximately 20 biscuits but alter quantities according to how many dates you have left-over.

- 200g plain flour
- 100g butter
- 75g chopped dates
- Grated nutmeg
- 75g caster sugar
- 3 egg yolks, beaten

Variations

- Figs

Christmas Pudding Crème Brulée

⏱ 10 ⏱ 40

This recipe uses up the remains of both the Christmas pudding and the cream that goes with it.

Always keep your Christmas pudding in an airtight container as this keeps it moist and therefore not too crumbly and it will last up to 6 months, improving with age. If it does start to dry out a bit, try adding a little bit of brandy, which will be soaked up by the pudding, making it rehydrate. Obviously, this is not advisable too many times or it may become a health hazard!

Leftovers used

Christmas pudding; cream.

Method

❶ Preheat the oven to 180°C/350°F/gas mark 4.
❷ In a saucepan, bring the cream, brandy and vanilla essence to the boil and then set aside.
❸ Divide up the Christmas pudding evenly between 4 large ramekins.
❹ Whisk up the egg yolks and sugar until fluffy and pale.
❺ Slowly combine the cream and vanilla essence with the eggs and sugar, stirring constantly. Then add the brandy and mix in.
❻ Pour the mixture into the ramekins so that there are equal amounts in each of them.
❼ Put the ramekins in a deep baking tray and fill the tray with water so that it reaches about ¾ of the way up the ramekins.
❽ Bake in the oven for about 15 minutes, until the mixture has just set.
❾ Take out and allow to cool for 20 minutes.
❿ Sprinkle soft brown sugar over the top of the puddings and put under a very hot grill until sugar melts and caramelises on the top. (Alternatively, use a mini blowtorch if you have one, which will produce more consistent results.) Serve either hot or cold.

Ingredients

- 200g Christmas pudding
- 250ml double cream
- 3 egg yolks
- 1 tablespoon caster sugar
- ½ teaspoon vanilla essence
- A dessertspoon brandy (optional)
- Soft brown sugar

Individual Recipes: sweet

Grilled Peaches with Cinnamon and Rum Sauce

🕐 10 🕐 10

The peach is just one of the fruits that is made for summer, but so often they are either bullet-like or they are left for just a fraction too long and get soft. Either way, this recipe will really pep up your peaches!

Peaches can be frozen in segments by removing the pit, slicing into halves or quarters, then placing them in a container and covering them with a sugar and water syrup. Adding ¼ teaspoon of lemon juice prevents them becoming discoloured. Make sure you use ripe peaches for freezing.

If you have some slightly bruised or over ripe peaches, purée them in a blender (removing the skins and pit first), add some sugar to the purée and freeze in an airtight container. This is ideal for defrosting and using in smoothies or juices.

This recipe is delicious served with thick double cream, crème fraîche or really good vanilla ice cream.

Leftovers used

Slightly hard or soft peaches.

Method

❶ Preheat the grill so it is really hot.

❷ Use a skewer to make a hole through each peach half and then thread a cinnamon stick through the hole so that there are two halves on each cinnamon stick, threading a mint leaf between each half.

❸ Brush the grill grate with oil and place the peach halves on the grate. Grill on both sides for 3-4 minutes until they are nicely browned.

❹ Meanwhile, melt the butter in a saucepan with the sugar, rum, salt and ground cinnamon. Bring to the boil and let it simmer for about 5 minutes until it thickens.

❺ Transfer the peaches onto a serving plate and pour over the sauce.

❻ Serve with a blob of crème fraîche or vanilla ice cream.

Ingredients

- 4 peaches, halved with pit removed
- 4 cinnamon sticks
- Fresh mint leaves
- 4 tablespoons unsalted butter
- 25g brown sugar
- 3 tablespoons dark rum
- ½ teaspoon ground cinnamon
- Pinch of salt

Iced Coffee

 5

If you have made a pot of **coffee** and it has gone cold, don't throw it away – iced coffee is a delicious and refreshing drink, especially during the summer. Served in a long glass, it can be drunk at any time of night or day.

Iced coffee can get watered down by the ice cubes. To avoid this, you can freeze small amounts of the coffee beforehand in an ice cube tray and put some of these in the glass with the ice before you pour.

There are literally hundreds of varieties of iced coffee that can be conjured up by adding a number of different flavours to the basic iced coffee ingredients.

For an iced latte, follow the recipe below but pour it into a glass half filled with cold milk. Try adding whipped cream on top of your iced coffee, together with a sprinkle of chocolate powder, to jazz it up a bit.

Ingredients

- 1 cup of cold black coffee
- Milk to taste
- Sugar to taste
- Ice cubes
- 1 drop vanilla essence (optional)

Variations

- Cinnamon and caramel sauce
- Cocoa powder and chocolate
- Pudding mixture
- Vanilla and almond extract

Leftovers used

Black coffee.

Method

❶ If you manage to catch the coffee whilst it is still lukewarm, add a teaspoon of sugar and stir well. If the coffee is already cold, warm it up slightly so that the sugar melts easily.

❷ Let the coffee and sugar mixture go cold and add the vanilla essence if using. If you want milk in your iced coffee, add as much as you need and stir well.

❸ Fill a tall glass with ice cubes, or coffee cubes and pour the iced coffee over the top.

Lemon Meringue Pie

⏱ 50 ⏱ 40

An old favourite but sometimes forgotten, it is one of the most resourceful puddings as it uses the whole **lemon**, juice and zest, and both the yolk and the white of the **eggs**. In addition, in this recipe I have used a biscuit base rather than a pastry base so you can use up the remains of a soft packet of digestive or ginger **biscuits**.

Leftovers used

Soft biscuits; egg whites; slightly old lemons.

Method

1 Preheat the oven to 180°C/350°F/gas mark 4 and grease a 23cm flan tin with a removable base.

2 Crush the biscuits – a food processor is quick and easy.

3 Melt the butter in a saucepan and add the sugar and biscuits and mix well.

4 Press the mixture into the base of the tin and put in the fridge to harden.

5 Meanwhile, mix the corn flour, sugar and lemon zest in a medium saucepan. Then strain the lemon juice through a sieve and stir in gradually.

6 Add the orange juice and cook over a medium heat, stirring constantly, until thickened and smooth.

7 Once the mixture starts to boil, remove from the heat and beat in the butter until melted. Beat the egg yolks and whole egg together, stir into the pan and return to a medium heat. Keep stirring vigorously for a few minutes, until the mixture thickens so that it does not run off the back of a spoon.

8 Take off the heat and after a few minutes, pour it over the biscuit base flattening it out evenly.

9 For the meringue whisk the egg whites until they form stiff peaks. Add half the sugar and whisk for another 30 seconds until the mixture looks shiny.

10 Fold in the remaining sugar and vanilla essence. Lay the meringue over the curd filling and cook in the oven for about 25 minutes until the meringue is browning on top. Allow to chill before serving. (You may have to run a knife around the edge of the tin before lifting the pudding out as the curd may stick slightly to the tin).

Ingredients

For the biscuit base
- 8 digestive biscuits (or ginger biscuits)
- 75g butter
- 4 tablespoons Demerara sugar

For the lemon curd filling
- 2 teaspoons corn flour
- 150g caster sugar
- Zest of two lemons
- 150ml freshly squeezed lemon juice
- 200ml orange juice
- 85g butter
- 1 large egg and 3 egg yolks

For the meringue
- 4 egg whites
- 200g caster sugar
- 1 teaspoon vanilla essence

Ingredients

- 175g butter or margarine
- 2 tablespoons golden syrup
- 180g Demerara sugar
- 250g muesli/stale cornflakes

Variations

- Chocolate coated flapjacks

Flapjacks

  10 30

Although you normally make flapjacks with rolled oats, muesli is just as good and gives a mixture of textures and tastes. Stale muesli is fine and if you have half muesli and half stale cornflakes, it's a great way to use up your cornflakes!

Oats and muesli are a great source of slow releasing energy so these are perfect for a mid-morning snack for adults and children.

Don't be tempted to overcook flapjacks, they are much nicer gooey! 30 minutes should be enough time as they will go on cooking even when they come out of the oven.

To jazz them up even further, pour some melted chocolate over the top and allow the layer to harden by chilling in the fridge. Store in an airtight biscuit tin.

Leftovers used

Stale corn flakes or muesli; rolled oats.

Method

1. Preheat the oven to 160°C/325°F/gas mark 2.
2. Melt the butter or margarine in a non-stick pan over a low heat. When it has melted, add the golden syrup and sugar and stir until it has all dissolved.
3. Take the pan off the heat and add the muesli or cornflakes and stir all the mixture until the ingredients are really mixed in well.
4. Line a shallow baking tray with greased baking parchment and pour the mixture onto the tray. Use a wooden spoon to press the mixture down evenly all over the tray.
5. Put in the oven and cook for 30 minutes.
6. When cooked, take out the tray and cut into squares in the tray whilst it is still hot (it's much easier to cut when still soft). Leave to cool for about an hour.
7. Transfer the squares into a cake/biscuit tin.

Meringues

🕐 15 🕐 180

Meringues will go with any pudding but try adding whipped cream and summer fruit on the top of each meringue to make them into a pudding in their own right.

The secret to successful meringues is long slow cooking at a low temperature; while you have the oven turned down low, make some extra to freeze. They freeze well – make sure you freeze them in a solid container to prevent them getting crushed in the freezer.

Makes 8-10 meringues (quantities can be adjusted according to how many **egg whites** you have leftover).

Leftovers used

Egg whites.

Method

❶ Preheat oven to 100°C/220°F/gas mark ¼.
❷ Grease two baking trays really well, or cut out a piece of greased cooking parchment to fit the baking trays.
❸ Put egg whites in a large bowl and whisk until they become firm and form little peaks.
❹ Add half the sugar and continue to whisk for about 30 seconds until the mixture looks 'silky'.
❺ Fold in the remainder of the sugar and the vanilla essence being careful not to lose the air in the whisked egg.
❻ Using a piping tube or a teaspoon, make little mounds of the mixture, well spaced apart on the baking tray.
❼ Place in the centre of the oven and cook for 3 hours until the meringues are hardened on the outside and faintly brown.
❽ Remove from the baking tray and cool on a cooling rack.
❾ Store in an airtight container.

Ingredients

- 4 egg whites
- 200g caster sugar
- 1 teaspoon vanilla essence

Individual Recipes: sweet

Mixed Fruit Cheesecake 15 🕐 50

A cheesecake is ideal for using up any slightly soft **biscuits**, including the crumbs from the bottom of the biscuit tin and it provides an opportunity to use up a variety of soft **fruit** as colourful decoration.

Traditionally, digestive biscuits are used for the base of a cheesecake but ginger biscuits are a really good alternative, or a combination of the two biscuits if you don't have enough of one type.

Any kind of soft fruit can be used for the topping.

Leftovers used

Fruit: raw apples, bananas, blackcurrants, blueberries, cherries, gooseberries, lemons, kiwi, raspberries and strawberries; soft biscuits.

Method

1. Preheat the oven to 180°C/350°F/gas mark 4.
2. Grease a 20cm cake tin.
3. Crush the biscuits between two pieces of kitchen towel, or in a food processor.
4. Melt the butter in a saucepan and add the sugar and biscuits and mix well.
5. Press the mixture into the base of the cake tin and put in the fridge to harden.
6. Beat the cream cheese, soured cream, flour, sugar, vanilla essence, eggs and yolk until the mixture is light and fluffy.
7. At this stage you can combine some fruit such as raspberries, strawberries or blueberries with the mixture if you wish.
8. Pour the mixture into the cake tin on top of the biscuit base and cook in the oven for about 40-45 minutes, until it has set but is still slightly wobbly. Allow to cool.
9. Meanwhile, prepare your fruit for the top of the cheesecake, picking out any fruit that does not look its best.
10. When the cheesecake is cool, decorate with fruit and sieve some icing sugar over the top if you wish.

Ingredients

- 8 digestive biscuits (or ginger biscuits)
- 75g butter
- 4 tablespoons Demerara sugar
- 500g full fat cream cheese
- 1 teaspoon vanilla essence
- 2 tablespoons plain flour
- 150g caster sugar
- 2 eggs plus 1 egg yolk
- 140ml pot of soured cream
- 150g fruit of your choice
- Icing sugar

Variations

Toppings
- Almonds
- Apples
- Cherries
- Grated chocolate
- Gooseberries
- Kiwi fruit

Scones

⏱ 10 ⏱ 10

It's very easy for **milk** to go slightly off, especially if you buy it in the big six-pint cartons. Although sour milk is disgusting in cereal or tea and coffee, it is ideal for scones, which are quick and easy to make and also fun for the children to do.

Plain or sultana scones are delicious with clotted cream and fresh jam, and where I live, in the West Country, it's jam first and then the clotted cream on top!

Savoury scones can also be made using the same recipe but adding about 50g of grated **cheese** instead of the sugar. Both types of scone will freeze well.

Leftovers used

Slightly sour milk.

Method

① Pre-heat the oven to 230°C/450°F/gas mark 8. Grease two baking sheets with butter or margarine.
② Sift flour, baking powder and salt into a bowl. Cut up the butter or margarine into the flour and rub it into the flour using your fingertips.
③ Add the sugar, milk and sultanas, mix to a soft dough and mould it into a ball.
④ Roll out the dough on a floured worktop until it is about 1 cm thick.
⑤ Using a 6cm diameter round cutter cut the dough into circles. Squeeze the scraps into a ball and repeat until all the dough has been used.
⑥ Put the circles on the baking sheets, leaving about 5cm between each one.
⑦ Brush the tops with milk and bake in the oven for 7-10 minutes until the scones have risen and turned golden.
⑧ Lift them onto a wire rack to cool.
⑨ Serve with butter or clotted cream (optional) and strawberry jam.

Ingredients

(Makes about 16 scones)

- 225g self-raising flour
- 1 teaspoon baking powder
- Pinch of salt
- 50g butter or margarine
- 25g caster sugar
- 150ml milk (slightly 'off' milk can be used)
- 50g sultanas (optional)
- Extra milk for glazing

Variations

- Savoury cheese scones

Summer Fruits Frozen Yoghurt

⏱ 15

Ingredients

- 500g any combination of summer fruit
- 150g caster sugar
- 500g whole milk natural yoghurt; or half natural yoghurt and half strawberry/raspberry yoghurt

Summer berries are such a treat but can often be expensive, especially if you buy berries slightly out of season in supermarkets, when they are often less tasty than locally grown seasonal berries as a result of being grown in an artificial environment and, in some cases, having been chilled and transported half way around the world.

If you do happen to grow your own fruit, you may end up with a glut around August, when fruit is also at its least expensive in the shops, so this is an ideal time to freeze any surplus. You can freeze berries by laying the fruit out on a flat tray in the freezer and transferring to a freezer bag when frozen.

This recipe is perfect for just about any type of summer berry. Blackberries can be picked for free from the hedgerows, and can be combined with slightly more tart berries such as blackcurrants, strawberries or raspberries to give a really big berry taste! Don't worry if your fruit is a little soft as the berries are puréed and sieved.

Leftovers used

Blackberries, blackcurrants, blueberries, raspberries, strawberries.

Method

1. Warm the fruit in a saucepan with the sugar until the juices are released from the berries.
2. Purée the fruit (in a processor if you have one) until smooth.
3. Pass the fruit through a sieve, collecting the juice and fruit pulp in a large bowl.
4. Stir in the yoghurt until it is well mixed with the puréed fruit.
5. Put the mixture into a container and put in the freezer. When it is almost frozen, remove and whisk the mixture really well to remove any ice crystals. Repeat this a couple more times, about every hour, until the mixture is really frozen.
6. Or if you have an ice cream maker: transfer mixture to the ice cream maker and process until the yoghurt has frozen. Transfer to a sealable container and store in the freezer.

Summer Pudding

 20

Plus overnight to chill

This is one of those lovely fresh puddings that simply can't be beaten; the colour of summer pudding makes it utterly irresistible and it really is incredibly easy to make. You can make up the fruit filling with different soft fruits, depending on which are available, but try to avoid using too many blackberries, as they will make the pudding too dark.

This is also one of the few recipes which actually uses stale white **bread** in its whole form, and it is actually preferable to use slightly stale bread because, being dryer, it absorbs more of the fruit liquid.

It is a good idea to make a batch of puddings (perhaps small ones as opposed to one big one) when summer fruit is available in copious quantities, and freeze them for the winter time when we have cravings for summer berries.

Leftovers used

Slightly soft summer fruit: blackberries, blackcurrants, blueberries, raspberries, redcurrants; stale bread.

You will need a round 1 litre pudding bowl.

Method

❶ Remove all the stems from the fruit.

❷ Stew the fruit by placing it all in a big saucepan with the water and the sugar and cook gently over a medium heat for about 3-5 minutes. Leave to cool.

❸ Line the bowl with the slices of bread, making sure you overlap them and press down hard to seal any gaps.

❹ Put half a cup of juice from the stewed fruit to one side.

❺ Pour the fruit and the remaining juice into the bread-lined bowl.

❻ Cover the top with another slice or two of bread.

❼ Put a plate that fits neatly into the top of the bowl on top of the bread and put something heavy on the plate to weigh it down.

❽ Place the bowl in the fridge, on a large plate (to catch any stray juice). Leave overnight so that the bread soaks up the juices.

❾ Before serving, turn out the pudding onto a large plate, spoon over the extra fruit juice.

❿ Serve with cream or natural yoghurt.

Ingredients

- 750g mixed summer fruit e.g. blackberries, blackcurrants, blueberries, raspberries, redcurrants
- 180g caster sugar
- 100ml water
- 7-8 slices of white bread from a large loaf (preferably slightly stale)

Tiramisu Ice Cream 5 5

While there are a large number of local companies making really delicious ice cream using good natural ingredients, it is fun and cheaper to make your own and you will know what has gone into it. This one is great for using up leftover strong **coffee**.

Ice cream is easy to make by hand, and even easier if you have an ice cream maker (see p.175). I keep mine permanently in the freezer so that it is ready to use at any time.

Ingredients

- Leftover espresso or strong coffee (about 100ml)
- 75ml port or sherry
- 4 large scoops really good vanilla ice cream (see opposite page)
- 75g dark chocolate

Leftovers used

Espresso coffee.

Method

1. Heat the espresso coffee and the port or sherry in a saucepan and simmer for a couple of minutes.
2. Meanwhile, put one large scoop of ice cream in each of four chilled dessert bowls.
3. Pour over the hot espresso mixture and grate the dark chocolate over the top.
4. Serve immediately.

Vanilla Ice Cream

 30

There are ordinary vanilla ice creams; and there are really good ones where the vanilla taste jumps out at you and there are no nasty ingredients or E-numbers. This is a really great way to use up **egg yolks** if you've just made a batch of meringues.

You will need 2-4 hours freezing time.

Leftovers used

Egg yolks.

Method

1 Whisk the egg yolks with half of the sugar until light and golden, in a large heat resistant bowl.

2 Place the creams and remaining sugar into a saucepan. Scrape the seeds from the vanilla pods into the creams and heat but do not allow to boil.

3 Remove from the heat and allow to cool slightly.

4 Gently stir the heated cream into the beaten egg, do not add too quickly otherwise the eggs might begin to cook and form scrambled eggs!

5 Place the bowl over a saucepan of simmering water and stir with a wooden spoon until the mixture thickens enough to coat the back of the spoon.

6 Remove from the heat and allow to cool.

7 Place in an ice cream maker and process until the ice cream begins to freeze. Transfer to a container and store in the freezer.

8 If you don't have an ice cream maker place in an airtight container and freeze for 2-4

Ingredients

- 110g (4oz) caster sugar
- 6 egg yolks
- 450ml single cream
- 450ml double cream
- 1 vanilla pod

Treacle Tart

⏱ 10 ⏱ 25

These days traditional puddings seem to have been cast aside somewhat in favour of slightly more trendy and exotic recipes. However, very few of the trendy puddings use up leftovers in the same way as the traditional ones – which was one of the main reasons for them being invented in the first place.

If you have lots of lovely **breadcrumbs** in the freezer you can make this recipe in the blink of an eye. What's more, treacle tart is ideal for freezing.

Ingredients

- 350g shortcrust pastry
- 120g breadcrumbs
- 135g golden syrup (about 8 tablespoons)
- Grated rind and juice of 1 lemon
- 1 tablespoon of orange juice (optional)

Leftovers used

Stale bread (breadcrumbs).

Method

❶ Preheat the oven to 200°C/400°F/gas mark 6.
❷ Grease a 10 inch pie/flan dish, roll out your pastry so that it is slightly bigger than the flan dish and place over the dish. Use your fingers to press down the pastry around the edges of the dish. Cut the excess pastry around the edge of the dish and prick the bottom of the dish with a fork in several places. (This allows air to get in whilst the pastry is cooking).
❸ Melt the golden syrup in a saucepan; add the lemon rind and juice, orange juice and breadcrumbs. Mix well and then pour the mixture onto the pastry.
❹ Roll out the remaining pastry case and cut into strips; use these to create a lattice design on the top of the tart.
❺ Cook in the middle of the oven for about 25 minutes until the pastry is crisp and golden.
❻ Serve with double cream or ice cream.

Index of Recipes

Also available from Green Books:

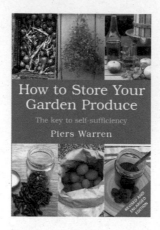

This easy household guide tells you everything you need to know about composting, from the different containers that are available, and what to put in them, to how to use your compost and what to do if you want to get more involved in the process.

Composting: an easy household guide includes an A-Z on how to compost everything from ash to weeds; advice on how to compost in small spaces, information on bins and wormeries and getting more involved in bigger community schemes.

ISBN 978 1 903998 78 6
£4.95 paperback

"Every serious organic gardener should have a copy" – *Organic Gardening* magazine

The modern guide to storing and preserving your garden produce, enabling you to eat home-grown goodness all year round. In the A-Z list of produce, each entry includes recommended varieties, suggested methods of storage and a number of recipes. Everything from how to make your own cider and pickled gerkhins to how to string onions and dry your own apple rings.

ISBN 978 1 900322 17 1
£7.95 paperback

What do you do with your old mobile phone? Where can you take your old medicines? Which plastic is recyclable? What happens to the stuff you recycle?

This easy-to-use guide has the answers to all your recycling questions. Use its A-Z listing of everyday household items to see how you can recycle most of your unwanted things, do your bit for the planet, and maybe make a bit of money while you're at it.

ISBN 978 1 903998 93 9
£4.95 paperback

For a complete list of our books, see www.greenbooks.co.uk